SYLVAN CRONE

Going Feral: Field Notes on Wonder and Wanderlust
Wolf Tree: An Ecopsychological Memoir in Essays

Sylvan Crone

A MIDLIFE QUEST

ESSAYS BY

Heather Durham

Published in 2025 by Wayfarer Books
Cover Design and Interior Design by Connor Wolfe
Cover Image © Weheartbotanics
TRADE PAPERBACK 978-1-965320-32-7
Interior Illustrations by © StudioRoux
10 9 8 7 6 5 4 3 2 1

Look for our titles in paperback, ebook, and audiobook wherever books are sold. Wholesale offerings for retailers available through Ingram.

Wayfarer Books is committed to ecological stewardship. We greatly value the natural environment and invest in conservation.

PO Box 1109, Abiquiú New Mexico

413.441.7003 | orders@homeboundpublications.com

WAYFARERBOOKS.ORG

Someday, I hope to be an elder. To be ready, I need to take the world into my body and keep it there in neat bundles of words.

—KIM STAFFORD, *THE MUSES AMONG US*[1]

When I imagine myself as that wise old woman with deep vision, I imagine myself not in a cave—but in a solitary little cottage in the middle of an enchanted forest, guarded by wolves and surrounded by a fence made of bones and skulls.

—SHARON BLACKIE, *HAGITUDE*[2]

Table of Contents

Land Acknowledgment

I am not of this place.

Roots in New England, I grew up among deciduous woodlands of sugar maple, red oak, and beech. Dug in to rocky granitic soils, caught tadpoles in vernal pools, floated in warm lakes, and balance-beamed along stone walls. I played hide and seek in tidy cornfields, climbed apple trees, and drank cider on hayrides through pumpkin patches. Caught fireflies in mason jars, scratched mosquito bites and poison ivy rashes, reveled in thunderstorms, and shoveled wet snow.

Though several generations of ancestors called New England home, we are not from there either. My people are from England, Scotland, far northwestern Europe. For hundreds, perhaps thousands of years, my people were indigenous to, wandered, rooted, and belonged in places I've never been.

I am not from here, but this is my home.

Home is the Cascadia bioregion, Pacific Northwest Coast. Rain country, river country, conifer forested rugged mountain country. Salmon runs and elk herds, ravens and wolves, spotted owls and bald eagles. Indians, settler colonialists, trappers, miners, loggers, farmers, tech workers, and sociopathic naturalist hermits.

Within the Cascadia bioregion, in northern Washington state, the North Cascades Ecosystem carves out a unique niche. South of the Fraser River, west of the Columbia River plateau, north of the Snoqualmie River, and east of the Salish Sea, from sea level to upwards of 10,000 feet, the North Cascades is defined by a complex geomorphological mashup of volcanism, glacial sculpting, and steep uplifted metamorphic peaks. Volcanoes, still active—Mt. Baker and Glacier Peak—glaciers, still sculpting—the most active glaciers in North America outside of Alaska— and mountains, still rising—dozens of pointy peaks with an average elevation of 7000 feet, nicknamed the American Alps.

Because of the rainshadow effect, wherein coastal moisture wrings out against this jagged mountain wall, an average of eighty inches of rain and snow fall annually across the ecosystem. This abundant moisture sustains alpine and subalpine forests and heather meadows, Douglas fir and riparian forests, and saturated dripping mossy fern-carpeted temperate rainforests.

Within the North Cascades Ecosystem, on the western foothills edge, my home nestles deep in "Ish" River country. Washington poet, Robert Sund:

> "Ish River"—
>> like breath,
>> like mist rising from a hillside.
> Duwamish, Snohomish, Stillaguamish, Samish,
> Skokomish, Skykomish… all the ish rivers.

I live in Ish River country
between two mountain ranges where
many rivers
run down to an inland sea.[3]

I live in Ish River country, in the Snohomish River highlands, the land of the Snohomish people for upwards of ten thousand years and still today. People of salmon, raven, coyote, eagle, bear, and elk. People of cedar, berries, canoes, longhouses, and rich culture. Just one of dozens of Coast Salish cultures, still here. In the language of my home, Ish means river.

In the Snohomish River highlands equidistant from the Stillaguamish and the Skykomish, at 600 feet above sea level on the western slope of 5000-foot Mt. Pilchuck, a small creek flows into the Pilchuck river. Just upriver from this confluence at the end of a pot-holed gravel road bordering a forgotten feral woodland where one might walk off into the Mt. Baker-Snoqualmie National Forest never to be seen again, an open circle of towering conifers hugs a tiny red cabin.

Outside this cabin, I sit against the grandmother cedar tree. She stands where the driveway meets the porch, the biggest cedar around, tall and straight yet somehow escaped the crosscut saw. Her branches like arms reach over my roof and her roots weave a foundation under my floor. She greets me when I come home, when I come outside, when I sit and stay and breathe. She reaches out with her scent, the sweet, lung-expanding, clearing, cleansing balm of Ish river country.

Or, I sit against the Douglas-fir tree. One of the dozen or so spanning the property, all planted, I was told, in 1930. Not the largest, but somehow, the dominant fir. The one around which the former owner had placed an elven statue and a flower pot tucked into a protruding encircling root which now grows a heather plant. The fir with a natural scoop out of the root base on the downhill side that makes the perfect perch from which to look out across the sloping mossy meadow through tufts of sword ferns to scattered spindly alders and a rushing creek below. Behind me, chickadees, juncos and jays work the feeders above. Douglas squirrels clean up below. Pacific wrens guard their own sword fern patches and pacific chorus frogs *creee-eek* from shadows unseen. Sometimes, an eagle flies in to survey the scene and I survey the eagle. This fir tree, at the central point of the property, is where it all happens.

Or, I sit in the place I was drawn to immediately upon seeking and finding this property as my home, the place that may be away from the house and away from the center but nevertheless feels like the heart of this landscape—the creek. My own little Ish with spawning coho and pink salmon, wading dippers, diving kingfishers, and skulking coyotes. I sit in the iron chair against the moss and lichen-covered cedar stump growing a hemlock sapling. I sit with my rubber boots in the water because the creek is flooded again. I sit robed in rain gear and rain hat because it's raining again, but I can't hear the rain over the sound of the rushing creek. If I sit there long enough the Ish obliterates all else—my rushing thoughts, my very sense of self, until all that is left is the little forest clearing embraced by cedar and fir, squirrels and songbirds flitting about, ravens above announcing bear and bobcat roaming the forest to the east, and the ceaseless Ish River in the rain.

I am not of this place, but I am home.

I

Mother

Biological clock? I never got it. I mean, I understand the phrase as a concept, but I don't *get* it, not as they said I was supposed to. Not as they assured me I would, when the time came. Which is part of the definition, I guess, that when I reached a certain age it would be time, *tick, tick, tick*—that my body would make that abundantly clear. That one day, babies would be these needy wriggling fragile screaming little lumps and the next they'd transform into charming effervescent delicate cooing little angels and that I'd want, no, *need* one of my own so badly I would ache with that need.

I guess what I'm really talking about here is baby fever. I never got it. In fact, the closer I come to spinsterhood, the more comfortable, even relieved I am that I never had it. Neither the fever, nor the baby.

It's not that I dislike children. Children are just little people, and as far as people go, I take them on a case-by-case basis. I spent my young adult life working with children—teaching at outdoor schools and nature centers. It was rewarding work, even fun sometimes when I was able to stop worrying about them and how I was doing and what I could be doing better and what I should do differently next time. Mostly, I worried. I was always relieved to hand them back over to someone else. I still don't generally enjoy finding myself in large groups of children due to my increasing aversion to noise, disorder, and various manifestations of distress (which translates to adult crowd aversion too).

Of course, I have known and know many delightful, fascinating, marvelous, heart-melting little people who enrich my life just like some of the big ones. That just never translated into the desire to make one of my own, and certainly not to be responsible for raising one. I find the thought terrifying.

But babies, as I understand the urge centers around—*babies??* I don't get that at all. A naturalist friend of mine recently asked me which animal babies I thought were the ugliest and without skipping a beat I said human. Give me a toothy opossum or a naked mole rat any day—those critters are cute. A coworker brought a baby goat into the office one day and I squealed and hand-waggled and shoved people out of the way to get my hands on the furry beastlet. But a shrill helpless little hominid? More likely to evoke a polite smile and bafflement. Why would anyone want one of those?

Some middle-aged woman I am. Some human.

You'll understand when you're a mother, my mother and mothers everywhere used to tell me. *You can't understand because you're not a mother*, my sister and mothers everywhere tell me now.

They're right. I can't, and I won't. And sure, I can recognize, logically, that I am missing out. Just as I missed out by not joining the Peace Corps, not backpacking around Europe, and not staying in one place doing one thing instead of spending my young adult life indulging a wanderlust that kept me moving in and out of jobs and homes and landscapes and relationships into my mid-forties, so that I barely knew where—or who—I was much of the time.

Now, after all that wandering and wondering, having finally slowed and settled down in a place I just might stay, as my body too slows and settles into middle age, I can finally, confidently say that I know where and, even, briefly, sometimes, who I am. And, who I am not. I am not a mother, nor will I ever be a mother. And I am happy about that.

And yet?

There is a deep-seated desire that got me where I am now, a curiosity that grew to an aching need full of envy and frenetic obsessing. It started in my early thirties. When many of my cohort were coupling up and settling down, I was breaking up and learning to live alone again. It was then that this strange new desire took root. Or rather, tiny tendrils sprouted, seemingly out of thin air, and began seeking somewhere to root. Not just anywhere, but a very specific sort of place.

I didn't want a baby, didn't want then didn't particularly care whether I found a husband or a wife, regularly sought, found, changed my mind about and re-sought meaningful work, but what I started to desire more than anything, what I began to ache for, was a home of my own.

This wasn't just a search for a homeland or region that felt like home, though I went through that too, bigtime. Wandering that began as adventuring and exploring newness and somehow became purposeful seeking, culminating in my deep bond with the Pacific Northwest. *Going Feral: Field Notes on Wonder and Wanderlust*[4], my mid-twenties to early-thirties coming of age walkabout that culminated in my finding my ecological niche. It seems my own biological clock was first and foremost connected with landscape.

And then, nearing the time when society and supposedly biology should make me want to have babies, I found myself newly single, starting over, and starting to fantasize about something else. In my journal from my mid-thirties, I found the first mention: *I'm going to find a cabin in the woods near a river.* That's it; just a single line, just a wisp of an idea, likely grounded in escape more than anything else. Running away instead of toward.

But four months later, the tendrils had grown and branched:

Soon I will live in a home by the river in the trees—my sacred land. I can see myself in the future, an old crone in my wood cabin on the river, reading, writing, thinking, dreaming.

River, trees, sacred. Crone in a wood cabin. Reading, writing, thinking, dreaming.

I only recently discovered how often I repeated that sentiment over the years since, so many of the details the same. I repeated it so often it almost became a mantra. Even, a spell. From my journals:

- *I will have my cabin in the woods with my beautiful sacred things.*

- *In the future I will have a friendly wooden cottage in a meadow near a stream (brook, river) from which I will go experience the world.*

- *One day I'll find a little cottage by the creek and will have the best of all worlds: water, forest, mountains, town, city.*

- *When I finally settle down in the Northwest I will have a cabin on a river.*

- *I need to live by a river of course. With trees of course. My cabin on a river with a garden and some cats.*

- *Sometimes I think trees are enough for me, then I come across an enchanted river and remember where I am really home. Clear water, just deep enough, smooth stones, mossy ferny banks, moving, rushing, ambling, sometimes roaring, but not too much of a hurry. I must remember this. It all comes back to rivers.*

- *In the dream it was the cabin in the woods and a few cats and I.*

- *When I am an old woman I will finally grow into my skin and claim the title "that crazy old witch with the cats." I won't need to hide the eccentric loony side but will wear it proudly with the smile lines on my sun spotty weathered old skin. I'll sit for hours watching the birds and the wind in the swaying old willow trees, a smiling old woman and her cats.*

- *I'm going to live on a river. I hope it's one with salmon in it.*

- *One day I will have my own adorable cabin on my land. And a long driveway just to me and a fence and long walkway so nobody, ever, will just drop in.*

- *I will find my long-term home, my soul's hearth. I will know it because it will be perfect. Peaceful, comfortable, solid, safe. Beautiful, sacred, wild. Cedar trees. A creek or river. Sunny meadow. Barred owls and coyotes. I will find it.*

- *I wandered for so long, and now I want my home, cabin on land on the outskirts. I want it so badly it hurts.*

At some point my journal fantasies became genuine desires, and those genuine desires walked out of my journal into my daily life. I started talking about it. Often more flippantly than seriously, because who was I kidding, my years of wandering, career-changing and mind-changing had left me with no savings, an earlier bankruptcy and later, a new accumulation of school loan debt. But those who knew me knew. I had the bug.

It just felt like something I had to do, some destiny I needed to fulfill in order to be my true self. Not the addictive neediness that had me bumbling into and out of human relationships that came with all sorts of wacky and changeable inclinations that seemed to have more to do with molding myself into the person I was with. My yearning for a home came on when I was alone and felt most grounded, most myself.

And yet it somehow wasn't just about me. I wasn't seeking safety or security, not in the traditional sense of those words. A near-broke middle-aged woman living alone in a rustic cabin in the woods isn't necessarily safe or secure.

The desire turned aching need was about relationship, about longevity, and about caretaking. I wanted a place, not a person, to care for. The cabin that would shelter me, yes, but also the earth that would hold us. Ancient trees I might protect from a chainsaw. Birds I could steward by allowing native plants to grow and flower, nurturing pollinators and other insects to feed them. Deer, coyotes, and bear I might welcome into those feral meadows, all of us welcome at the creek I would do my part to keep clean and shaded for the salmon.

After I had stopped working with kids, I spent years in jobs as tree planter, restoration ecologist, wildlife biologist, and naturalist, all of it spent stewarding landscapes and moving on. Literally planting trees and never returning to see them grow. I don't regret any of it. Just as I never regretted mentoring other people's children. But unlike the children, there came a time when I yearned to plant things and stick around. Watch them grow. Watch the whole web of life interact not as the general concepts of tree, bird, creek. Particular trees. Individual birds. One specific creek I would get to know intimately. And, get to stay with. Commit to, and protect from harm.

Once I had the idea, the picture in my head, I couldn't let it go. It became an almost physical ache, a homesickness for the home that wasn't yet mine. A place I needed to get back to, could see myself growing old in, just hadn't found yet. Every friend who bought a house was the object of my greenest envy. Every country drive was a chance to discover, to ogle new country homes. I sized up and weighed and wondered and imagined my way into countless woodland cabins on creeks and rivers throughout Oregon and Washington. The social media term *cabin porn* may have been created for me.

I was old and worldly enough to know that owning a home, owning land brings with it whole hosts of stressors that renters don't have. I'd enjoyed the ease of something breaking and getting to call a landlord to deal with (and pay for) it. I wasn't expecting ease. I was looking for something that had been missing in all those rented rooms and mother-in-law apartments. Even all those beautiful, peaceful woodland cabins

I'd lived in over the years. The thought of sitting under a cedar tree on a fern-laced hillside by a creek that I belonged to, where I would get to stay— that, I believed, would be worth all the stress, and the struggle.

That land and all its creatures were out there somewhere, waiting to be loved, and I so very much wanted to find it so I could start loving it back. To be the protector that landscape needed, but also, to let that land anchor me as I'd never felt anchored before. Finally, I felt ready for longevity. Commitment.

Psychology might say I have a misguided mothering instinct, as psychology might say to a woman deemed excessively attached to her pets or houseplants. Psychology might say I have maladaptive human relationship skills or an attachment disorder due to traumatic relationship experiences. Psychology is probably right.

And? I've learned to also listen to another voice—ecology. *Wolf Tree: An Ecopsychological Memoir in Essays*[5]. Ecology, by nature, is older and wiser than psychology. More worldly. Less the erudite professor and more the insightful elder grandmother.

I'm a human animal, in deep relationship with the earth. And whereas various species may have tendencies, even rules governing how they might normally move through the world, there are always rule breakers. Always alternate strategies for making a life on earth. Maybe my relationships don't always look like the ones prescribed for me in my culture, but I did reach a point in my life where it felt time to settle down.

Tick, tick, tick. After decades ruled by zugunruhe—migratory restlessness—I finally felt pulled more strongly by the opposite. It was nesting time. Root down and reassess time. Relationship and connection time. Not as mother or even partner, but a whole cadre of other definitions, just a fraction of all a middle-aged woman might be. And, who she might wish to become as she begins the path to elderhood.

2

Transient

Star Island Retreat Center

Cross the Atlantic to this New England island hermitage from your past. The passenger ferry might as well be a wooden ship, a portal to another time, a fairy passage to Avalon. You'll find stone cottages perched on granite, rocking chairs on creaky wooden porches, and white painted gazebos in the meadows. The perfect place for your newly divorced mother, baby sister and five-year-old you to get away from it all, spend a week in the salt air by the ocean, crouching in the wildflowers, picking mica from the rocks, and nibbling seaweed from the earth like feral animals.

Auerbach Farm

Nestle into this humble cottage at the end of a winding dirt road in pastoral New England. Though still a working farm, the former farm workers' dwellings are rentable, the ideal setting for a single mother and her two daughters to start over, complete with apple orchards, pumpkin fields, and milk cows. At the center of the sunny cottage stands an antique cast-iron stove you can cook on when the power goes out. A screened-in porch leads out to the meadow where an old tire swing hangs from the old maple tree, then miles of woodland beyond. Leave the garage door ajar to allow entry to your five cats, but beware the raccoons.

YMCA Camp Takodah

Deep in the deciduous woodlands of southern New Hampshire, twenty-one forest green painted cabins separate into three age divisions named after displaced Indian tribes—Penacook, Monadnock, and Cherokee—though you wouldn't understand the harm in that until much later. Get there early, find your cabin, and choose a top bunk away from the screen door. Shove your locking trunk under the bed on the slatted wood floor, roll out your sleeping bag above, and head back outside to the picnic table by the fire ring where before long you will be cooking hotdogs and making s'mores with your new friends. Follow the well-worn paths past the bathhouse, toward the flagpole, past the dining hall, by the nurse's station—you know the way—down the hill to the waterfront for the swim test so you can get cleared to go past the dock into the deep water during free swim. Rest in one of the rocking chairs and look out on the waters of your home away from home. For ten summers of childhood into young adulthood, your sanctuary, your retreat, your special place.

Fairytale cabin

Reach into your ancestral memories, your collective unconscious, your dreams. There was always a cabin in the woods. Grimm's

Fairytales, dark and not quite fit for children, magic lurking in the shadowy corners. *Snow White, Red Riding Hood,* even *Little House on the Prairie.* Once upon a time, there was always a cabin. A forest. A little girl or a woman and perhaps a witch or clever fox or wolf or any number of wild beasts because deep down, you know where you came from and where you belong. A tiny cabin in a northern village tucked into the trees by the water—that has always been your place.

Sargent Center for Outdoor Education

After college when many friends leave suburbia for the big cities, you retreat to another cabin in the forest—a wooden farmhouse-turned staff house for environmental education instructors. Bat roosts in the attic, mice infestations in the walls, slanted floors, and leaden windows requiring stout sticks to prop them open. Head out the back door past the staghorn sumac where the veery sings his throaty tune, to the wood-chipped path into the forest, over the swampland boardwalk, and along the ragged meadow to your first "real" job.

Thoreau's cabin

You know the one. You likely know the dimensions, can picture the writing desk in the corner and the bean field outside. The ponds, vernal pools and New England country roads, perhaps even a covered bridge on the way to town. You know it so well, it's as if you lived there too.

Tracy Aviary

Unlock three padlocks and muscle open a fifteen-foot barbed wire-enforced gate that keeps the rest of Salt Lake City out and a menagerie of birds and you in this protected corner of Liberty Park. Crunch the gravel pathways between owl cages, among the wandering waterfowl, past the eagles to a two-room office-turned-intern dwelling, more shack than cabin. Away from the human noise and chaos of the city, in a grove of conifers and cages, revel in the avian noise and chaos of a world of birds. Sleep beneath a rooftop Indian peacock. Wake to the reveille of a Chinese rooster, and chuckle at the ongoing parrot soap opera next door. Daytimes, hide out from the humans and chat with the birds as you clean cages and fill food bowls.

Breitenbush Hot Springs Retreat Center

Leave another crowded city and a failed relationship for a one-room Thoreauvian cabin just for you, complete with a log ladder up to a sleeping loft where you can only sit up in the middle. Your tiny cabin perches on the edge of an off-grid village of other tiny cabins along the Breitenbush River deep in the rainforest wilderness of the Oregon Cascades. The cabins, lodges, dining hall, and meeting yurts and the paths that connect them form an archetypal village that feels like home the first time you visit and holds after you move there. Humble human structures, Adirondack chairs and cedar benches, footbridges, frayed prayer flags, and stone cairns all look so natural, so right, it's as if they grew there under the trees and amidst the wildflowers. Every detail purposeful, lovingly arranged and lived in, on a scale we know and remember in our ancestral memories.

Boulder, Colorado mother-in-law cabin

Start over all over again in this genuine, honest to goodness one-room log cabin in the Rocky Mountain foothills. Park in the landlord's driveway then follow the dusty footpath toward a tiny canyon where, in a grove of ponderosa pines, the cabin is built into the side of the ridge. Deeper into the canyon you'll find a stand of aspen trees along a gurgling creek. Inside the cabin you'll find a tiny propane fireplace and large double-paned windows. From there, you and your cat watch snowstorms, thunderstorms, mule deer, and even, twice, mountain lions.

North Cascades log home

One hour from the nearest grocery store, two hours from your preferred health food coop, in a town with a sign that reads "last services for 75 miles," which is only true about half the year when the mountain pass is even open, cross the Skagit river then the Cascade River to the dead-end gravel road with the two-story three-bedroom log house that costs the same to rent as would a one-room apartment in Seattle. Despite the drafty windows, moldy firewood, and mice infestations, you feel close to something there. In the solitude of the bigleaf maples and western redcedars, near the swollen rivers churning with salmon. Sitting on the wood floor of your covered porch, coffee mug warm in your hands and rain falling all around, you feel close to something like Home.

Forest Park cabin on the outskirts of Portland, Oregon

Retreat from too much isolation, yet another job that didn't stick, and the feeling that you haven't arrived yet, back to your favorite city. Not all the way back though, just to this communal hideout on the northern end of Forest Park, a 6000-acre protected forest also known as the Tualatin Mountains. Up the sloping driveway to the main house on the hillside orbited by five bedroom cabins within pastures of chickens, turkeys, and llamas or farther upslope under the firs. You live in the firs. Sit on the front steps by day and watch songbirds flock to your feeders. Sit on the front steps by night and spy on flying squirrels gliding down to your feeders. Listen to coyotes yowl and the barred owl family discuss what's for dinner.

Snoqualmie Valley, Washington tiny house

You're close now, in a job that hasn't yet made you restless, in a region that is close enough to wilderness but not too remote, close enough to progressive city culture but not too close to the crowds. This mother-in-law cottage, only 375 square feet so officially in the realm of Tiny Homes, could almost work. Wooden ladder up to a full-sized loft, large double-paned windows out to a ragged meadow where rabbits frolic, then miles of forest braided with creeks descending to the river valley below. Deer and coyotes wander through often. Elk and bear make cameos. Your hammock in the cedar grove offers deeper solitude.

And yet? You live there three years and manage to plant one lavender plant and one bedraggled rosemary, only because they get too big for their pots. Why root down, when you won't get to stay and grow? It isn't yours. It isn't Home. You won't get to live happily ever after, not here. But, you're close.

3

Goldilocks

A low, loud whine—like a gargantuan mosquito—brought me to the window. I peered through the screen and saw the apple tree moving, shaking, and shimmying alone on a windless September afternoon. Jonagold apples, the former owner had informed me, which I didn't know much about but which I was sure would be delicious, not least because that overgrown tree next to the gravel driveway now belonged to me.

I squinted into the foliage, tried to decipher what had animated my tree but all I could see were leathery leaves and almost-ripe apples. The tree stilled, afternoon quieted, and I returned to painting. I had a lot yet to do if I was going to start moving in over the weekend. I dipped the roller in the pan of sage-green paint and continued the joyful work of covering the dirt-brown wood paneling in the entryway, every stroke a light in the darkness, every brightened panel more mine than before.

I carried the same soft green into the open living room, then, rounding the corner, smoothed three coats of clean white over the rest of the dark paneling around the windows framing the mossy yard beyond. More white revived beige kitchen walls, and slate blue soothed anemic yellow cabinets. Up the iron spiral staircase to the open slant-roofed room that would serve as my bedroom at one end and writing nook at the other, I added an accent wall of lavender to contrast with the dark wood of my writing desk and the multilayered greens outside the windows toward the creek.

For the first time in my life, I got to choose every paint color; I didn't have to ask anyone for permission and would never have to put it back the way I found it. My colors, my sanctuary. Though I'd signed the final papers the week before, I still didn't quite believe it, was afraid I might awaken from a dream.

For the first time in my life, I wasn't squatting in someone else's space. I was beginning the process of creating in my own, and I could make it just right for me. The right combination of luck, timing, and privilege had finally made this deepest desire, this aching need come to pass. It felt like an impossible miracle. It still does.

The privilege part, wrapped up in luck and timing, was that I came into some money after the death of my stepfather. Long after. He'd died nearly ten years prior but the money had been held up in contentious legal issues surrounding the viability of the will and various family and other complications that made me give up on ever seeing any money, despite the fact that he'd left it to my sister and me. But suddenly, amazingly, thanks to my mother and a dear (step) uncle and aunt with integrity, there it was, just at the moment when that nesting urge had kicked into high gear.

What was left after lawyers had been paid out was just enough for a small down payment such that I might get a bank to give an otherwise broke but employed single woman a loan for a modest little property in the sticks, if I was willing to commute. I was willing to commute. For the right place, I was willing to sign a ream of paperwork to take on a new debt that made those school loan numbers look like pocket change.

I was willing to do a lot of driving, live paycheck to paycheck for the foreseeable future, and face the possibility of working into my seventies. But I was not willing to compromise. When I'd learned of my preapproval amount from the mortgage broker, I was told that I may be looking for a while. When I listed off my requirements to the husband/wife Realtor team, they told me it wasn't *impossible*, but I would need to be patient.

I was fine with that. I didn't just want a house; I wanted my cabin in the woods by the creek. Nothing fancy, but with basic amenities like plumbing and electricity, and solid enough that it wouldn't need any major work in the near future when I'd be particularly broke. A few large trees would be great, like western redcedar, Douglas-fir, or bigleaf maple. Bonus points for end of the road and/or wilderness adjacent. Bonus points for sunny meadows, a garden plot, fruit trees. Bonus points for porches, at least one covered. Heck, if we're getting picky, why not throw in a shed or garage for storage. Salmon and American dippers (water ouzels) in the creek. Coyotes, bobcats, and bears in the forest. Owls in the conifers. Why not?

I could wait. Had been waiting already, but now that my home was within reach, I was simultaneously calmed and invigorated. Instead of coveting the homes of friends and strangers, of ogling houses from the road or imagining fairytale cabins, I started to search real listings of available properties.

In my region, in my price range, there wasn't much. A lot of properties that fit, but without dwellings on them or with unlivable shacks or trailers that would require more money and skill than I had to live there. I'd roughed it before, lived in tents for months at a time, but in my late 40s looking for a long-term home, I was aiming for a certain modicum of comfort.

I found several almosts—a lovely cabin but so off-the-grid that it required a full-time generator and gathering water from the creek. A log home that would need most of its logs replaced before passing any inspection. An adorable and lovingly built tiny home in a lakeside forest, but squeezed in so tightly among other lakeside cabins so as to resemble a summer camp village—charming at a summer camp full of friends, repellant for a solitude-seeker among strangers. And mountain cabins that were exactly that—up in the mountains, requiring an extensive commute in good weather and the likelihood of months of winter driving at best and getting snowed in for weeks at a time at worst.

I mapped and researched details of potential properties online, and my Realtors and I exchanged weekly emails, clarifying and quickly discounting all I saw. They encouraged me to at least start visiting properties, to attend open houses and get an on-the-ground sense of what was out there, to perhaps refine what I was looking for. Maybe, lower my standards, or at least, broaden them?

They soon realized I wouldn't budge, and stopped sending me listings for suburban ranch houses with squared-off lawns that I barely looked at. I wasn't interested in wasting time trying on homes that weren't a good fit for me. I'd lived in, tried on, and tried out enough dwellings to know what would fit. I knew what I wanted and believed I would recognize it when I saw it, even on a computer screen.

I was right.

Outside, my apple tree shimmied and swayed, and, paintbrushes now soaking in warm soapy water, I stepped out on the front porch to get a better look. I didn't see anything immediately, so sat on the wooden steps next to the giant grandmother cedar tree that stretched tall next to the steep roof of the red-painted cabin.

Beyond the cedar, thick moss carpeted the earth at the end of the gravel driveway. On the other side of the driveway, the apple tree stood between a fenced-in feral garden plot and a towering Douglas-fir tree at the edge of a mixed coniferous/deciduous forest that stretched on for miles toward the Cascades Mountains. To the south, a sunny meadow punctuated by sword fern and huckleberry stump islands was ringed with ripe thimbleberry bushes. To the north, a line of firs shaded more moss and ferns down to my cheerful creek, whose gurgling I could hear from anywhere on my property and inside whenever the windows were open.

My property. My home.

Cabin in the woods by a creek. The property was listed on a Thursday; I discovered it online three hours later and made an appointment for the first time I had available—Monday. When I saw it, I knew.

The cabin was old, musty, quirky, and would need work, but seemed solid, livable, and friendly looking from the outside, like a storybook cottage. I could see myself there. Outside, amidst the conifers, moss, and ferns, I was already completely at home. Didn't want to leave.

The Realtors and I ate thimbleberries from the property as we walked around. I surreptitiously left a geode crystal in one of the stumps. Picked up a stone from the creek and put it in my pocket. Little magics to seal the deal. But it was already sealed, wasn't it? It was love at first sight in the way I used to believe in with people. You could practically hear the fanfare soundtrack, the Disney music, the dark skies parting and sunbeams shining down and all of it.

I made an offer that evening and accepted the counter-offer Wednesday morning. The first and only property I'd ever visited on my search and it was the one. Three weeks later, inspections completed (worry about all the work needed later), paperwork signed (and signed, and initialed, and signed, and initialed, and signed...), bank account emptied (worry about that later), I held the keys to happily ever after. And now, I sat on my front porch, looking out on my land, at my apple tree.

Chickadees *dee-dee*-ed from the firs above, nervous about something. An apple dropped, *thunk*, onto the grass.

And then, from the shadows, a yearling black bear trundled out, snuffling loudly, found the apple, and sat down munching. She was small, like a medium sized dog, with dark fur and a lighter snout, and she lay with paws in front of her like a child's stuffed animal. The tree still shook though, so I squinted until I recognized that same black coffee fur showing through windows in the dense foliage—another young bear feeding in the tree. If I strained, I could hear the crunching sounds, could envision sweet apple juice dribbling down their chins, the pulp, seeds, and skins gulped down together.

I didn't want to scare them, wanted them to continue to feel comfortable on my land so I went back inside, returned to cleaning and preparing for my move. But I did want to keep tabs on them so I returned to the window to open it wider. The window stuck for a moment then slammed open against the frame, making a loud noise I hadn't intended. I froze, looked out to see baby bear looking in my direction and the tree stilled. A moment later a large, bear-sized bear lumbered out of the forest and looked toward the house. Momma bear.

They looked. I looked. They sniffed. I smiled.

Then the three bears went back to eating apples. Alternately standing up on hind legs, climbing into the tree, lying around eating, and dozing in the shade, like they owned the place. Like they did this every year. And once I had that thought, I recognized proof in the apple tree, the way certain branches had bent, broken and healed from successive bear climbs. I'd later notice grooves in the bark, years of healed scratches and scars. My cabin in the woods had come with three bears.

I guess that makes me Goldilocks. Which has technically been true, most of my life, when I wasn't hiding under the punky crimson dyes of my twenties and the attempts at natural orange-red hennas of my thirties. Like it or not—mostly not, for all the societal baggage that goes along with it—I'm a blonde. But that doesn't mean I need to be that oblivious stereotype, that one-dimensional storybook character, that societal dummy who moves in and does what she wants, takes what she wants regardless of who I'm taking from. That may be an uncomfortable element of my ancestry, my cultural legacy, but it doesn't need to be how I live, here, now.

I hope to become a wise, white-haired elder who asks first, listens, adapts, and aims always for gentle harmony. Right now, I'm somewhere in between. Reaching middle age, I occasionally dwell in equanimity, but am still too often disparaging and stubborn, angry and petulant. Fading gold with some silver weaving in, and still, I realize, a long way from wisdom.

Over that next week, as I moved in and cautiously moved past the apple tree, the three bears would eat all the Jonagold apples. But I was coming to realize, they were more their apples than mine. Sure, some human had planted that tree long ago, and the paperwork I'd signed said it now belonged to me. But this land and the forest around it had been overseen, tended, inhabited, and owned by those bears and their ancestors long before any human, indigenous or colonizer, had. As a human animal I was still, in a way, squatting on this land. In my first week of inhabitance those bears were there to remind me of that.

I want to remember. To earn my place at the table, to steward and protect the property in partnership with the wild inhabitants. Not to own, but to serve. Our land, our home. Maybe next year they would leave me at least a few apples.

4

Grandmother

I don't remember the first time I met the western redcedar. It must have been sometime around the turn of the millennium when I first moved west to Oregon. Fresh from graduate school in environmental biology, I was awed and inspired by the Pacific Northwest forests. The colossal conifers, in particular, stood in stark contrast to the more humble, diminutive, leafy green trees of my northeastern upbringing. Whether I first distinguished redcedar in a field guide or in the naturalist training program I joined to help me get my bearings (and ideally, a job), I would have first learned the facts.

I learned that the correct common name is in fact "redcedar," not "red cedar," because *Thuja plicata* and its American cousins are not true cedars like the long-needled cedars of the old world. Instead, they are confusingly-named members of the cypress family of scaly-needled conifers.

I learned that the range of the western redcedar spans what I would later come to think of as my own ecological niche—low to middle elevation west side (wet side) forests of the Pacific Northwest, from British Columbia to northern California. If left undisturbed in their cool, shaded river valleys and creekside groves, they can grow to eight feet in diameter and two hundred feet high.

In the year 2000, I learned that western redcedars can live upwards of 2000 years, a fact that's easy to toss around until you really think about it, think about everything these ancient trees might have witnessed, what this landscape might have looked like and who might have known them as saplings. Certainly not any of my ancestors, off among the oaks on the British Isles.

As long as humans have been in this region, whether early Indigenous people or recent colonizers, we have been in relationship with the western redcedar. Not just in the way of most large trees—wood for tools, shelter, or fuel—though redcedar's rot-resistant, insect-repelling, clean-burning wood is excellent in that regard. Canoes, canoe paddles, totem poles, spear poles, arrow shafts, furniture, boxes, dishes, spoons, longhouse planks, little hermit cabin planks, firewood, and friction fire boards.

But also? Strips of fibrous bark or rootlets woven into baskets, nets, ropes, clothing, or shredded and worked into bedding, blankets, even diapers. Also? Resonant foliage steeped into teas or tinctures as antifungal, antibacterial, infection-fighting immune-stimulating medicine. And? Aromatic incense that energetically and literally (scientifically!) cleanses and purifies the air.

Western redcedar is this region's *Giving Tree*, the local Tree of Life. The uses, the facts abound. But sometime around the turn of the millennium, when I first began the process of sinking in to this region of rivers, ravens, and rain, redcedars were there with me, and I started to get to know them personally, intimately, viscerally.

In my forays outside of Portland I enjoyed hiking volcanic peaks and delighted in the rugged Pacific coast, but the forested rivers and creeks in between began to tug at me less from a yearning for adventure and more from a sense of homecoming. I explored many a trail along the Clackamas and Sandy Rivers, and along those trails would seek out just the right place to sit a while, maybe eat lunch, maybe scribble in my journal, bask in the sun with toes in the cool water or hunker down out of the cold rain depending on the season, and also, always, take some time to just sit, and breathe, and listen, and sink in to the forest, let the forest sink in to me. At my back, silent observer and solid support, was the western redcedar.

Warm cinnamon brown bark in vertical ripples, stood smooth and sturdy against my spine. A buttressed base with polished crimson roots spreading just above ground inevitably created nooks and hollows that fit a human body like a throne with armrests. Above, sprays of layered green scales fanned out in arcing waves, collecting raindrops or sashaying in the riverine wind.

Rivers are ancient, but on a human scale, cedars seem nearly as old. And if rivers drew cedars, it seems, cedars drew the rest of us. Sword fern, wild ginger, bleeding heart. Salmonberry, huckleberry, elderberry. Pacific wren, Swainson's thrush, Townsend's warbler. Pine marten, flying squirrel, coyote. We all came for these places redcedar created, the space they hold.

I sit with redcedar to find quiet. I sit there to find stillness. I sit there to shed the static electricity of the insular human world and remember my place in the wild one. Redcedar at my back—solid and steady, sweet-smelling and earth-bound.

Sitting there I start to get it. Sitting there I start to feel it, feel ego and self fade a little, allowing outside to seep inside. My breath a tree's exhalations. My exhalations a tree's breath.

I moved on to other rivers, other Cascadian rainforest watersheds. Snoqualmie, Skykomish, Skagit. There, I always found redcedar. Starting over with new jobs and new residences in new communities these friendly familiars helped orient and ground me. Coming home at the end of an overwhelming, frazzling day among my own baffling species I would seek out that one particular redcedar I'd chosen, or, perhaps, who'd chosen me, and get my bearings in the more-than-human world.

Redcedar's gifts extend beyond those riverside groves. Like many of those rooted in Pacific Northwest soil, I've lived in many a cedar plank home and warmed myself by clean-burning sweet-smoking redcedar fires. And, as a student of natural and cultural history, of deep nature connection that seeks direct experience beyond the facts, I dug in further. Tried my hand at friction fire, the "bowdrill" method that spun redcedar spindle into redcedar fireboard to create black dust and then a glowing coal that when added to shredded redcedar bark could be blown into flame. I wove bark strips into a traditional redcedar basket. I carved and sanded a redcedar branch into a spoon. I steeped redcedar needles into soothing tea for a chest cold. Tinctured needles in alcohol to make an immune-supporting, anxiety-calming, rash-dispelling medicine for my fiery disposition.

I don't remember when it happened, but *Thuja plicata* would no longer be just a tree with certain characteristics and uses. Redcedar refers to living, breathing, unique beings I've known, who've supported and sustained me and who've become an essential element of Home.

When I found my little cabin on the creek, I wasn't surprised, then, to find an ancient western redcedar standing at the center of the property, next to the front steps. Of course there was. Maybe that specific tree wasn't an essential item on my list— I would later discover several others from sapling to elder scattered around the property and into the forest. But this one, likely hundreds to over a thousand years old, stood by the front steps and told me: *Yes, this is the place for you.*

Her branches reach over my roof and roots weave under my floor, holding my fifty-four-year-old house and forty-nine-year-old me in a loose embrace. Whenever I return home, she is there to greet me, her perfume washing over me as soon as I step out of my car, my hand brushing her weathered skin in greeting as I walk up the steps. When I am frazzled or upset, happy or calm, angry or confused, I can sit with her and feel content to be whomever I happen to be.

Others, too, are drawn to her. Red-breasted sapsucker *tap-tap-taps* dotted lines of sap wells along her trunk so that her bark appears as an ancient hieroglyphic text. Douglas squirrel strips paper-thin bark from her outer branches to line a winter nest. Barred owl perches hidden in her foliage to stalk a deer mouse blundering into the open. Wild strawberries crowd around her base, the primary location I've found them on the property. These are just a few of those I've observed so far, though I know countless other lives have lived in, among, around, above and below my redcedar. I look forward to witnessing more of them, to understanding her multitudes better in the time we have together.

I know. It's just a tree, right? What kind of loony tree-hugger nonsense is this, right? Go out and find some real friends, right? Or maybe, at least, get some cats already? I know. I hear you. And yet...

I made a new tincture last spring, snipping green tips of redcedar foliage into alcohol and infusing it for six weeks. The resulting liquid is a green-amber concoction that unlike many medicinal tinctures, retains the strong cedar smell and taste. I siphoned it into dropper bottles, labeled them, then squirreled my medicine away in the cupboard for when I might need it.

Just two months later, I needed it.

I'd been outside standing on a rickety ladder left with the house, more comfortable than I should have been, more careless than I should have been. Painting, touching up some of the worn and stained redcedar house planks using a free gallon of paint also left with the house. As I reached up, leaned a little to the side, the old ladder shifted, twisted out from under me, and I fell.

Unlike the typical ladder-fall injuries involving bumps and bruises on the lucky end and head injuries or worse at the unlucky end, my fall and resulting injury took a unique turn. Falling, I reached an arm under me to break my fall and caught it in a thin electrical cord pulled taut between the house and a metal grounding rod.

The rest of my body's bumps and bruises were minimal. My arm—sliced open like a block of cheddar on a cheese cutter.

An ER visit, tetanus shot, morphine shot, several shots of Novocain, twenty-seven stitches and an antiseptic bandage later, I'd thought the worst was over. Soon afterwards, though, I developed a severe skin allergy to the chemical bandage, leaving my stitched-up arm looking even more like a bad makeup job from a slasher movie—Technicolor bruised, scarlet blistered, swollen and spurting various fluids at any moment.

I am intensely grateful for medical doctors and nurses, pharmaceutical pills and ointments, and health insurance. I am thankful for my neighbor who drove me to the ER, and coworkers who picked up my slack at work. Returning home to an empty house, however, drugged out and still feeling the most uncomfortable mashup of pain and intense itching I've ever experienced, made this loner hermit reevaluate her situation. It forced me to ask all the what-ifs and consider worst case scenarios, even if I'm not normally the type to do that when it comes to my own health and safety.

Did I yearn for someone to hold and comfort me, to cook and clean for me in my convalescence? To open jars and cans and all the other mundane tasks I never realized can be near impossible with only one working arm? To help me shower, clean and rebandage my tattered arm to save me from my awkward shoddy attempts? Or at the very least, at the beginning, to come running when I fell, pick me up off the ground, bring rags to apply pressure and dial the phone so I didn't have to manage that myself, adrenalated and bloody?

I probably should have. Might have, once upon a time in my younger days. But I didn't. The thing about loner hermits is, we get used to picking ourselves up off the ground and doing what needs to be done. Maybe, we don't remember any other way.

Also, I didn't feel alone—not the way I used to in my insular, human-focused youth. That redcedar tree keeping watch over me, my house, and this land—she did comfort me. Not in the way of my own species, but in her own ways. Drug-addled and broken, I sat with her, and she held me, that ancient grandmother, familiar and friendly, sweet, solid, and strong at my back. Her weathered skin against my bandaged arm, her medicine in my steaming tea.

Yes, she's just a tree. And I'm just a human, a relative newcomer to this landscape and this earth, a mere sapling rooting in her shade. We two living, breathing beings are in relationship now. And if that makes me a loony tree-hugger, so be it.

5

Witness

She didn't see me. A coyote trotted by me so closely I could have blown in her ear, and she didn't see me.

I was in the front of the house and happened to look through the glass door, across the yard, and through a window framed by the cedars and vine maples. There she was, making her way up the gravel road. Relaxed body posture, black-tipped ears alert, bushy tail trailing, bouncing along in the purposeful gait of a wild canine who knows her place and has a destination in mind, with both the haughtiness of a predator and the vigilance of prey.

I flew out the door intending to head up the driveway to maybe catch her disappearing into the woods, as her trajectory suggested. I paused for a moment, listening, feeling the afternoon sun on my face. I had just started my own purposeful trot across the porch when I saw her. I froze.

She hadn't continued into the forest, but had followed the gravel as it curved into my driveway, and continued to follow it toward my front porch, where I was standing.

I stayed frozen.

She kept trotting. Head slightly lowered, eyes on the ground ahead of her, ears perked, chestnut fur undulating over her shoulders and hips as she ambulated in my direction. Steady, determined, experienced gait, as if she knew the route. As if she did it every day.

Just as she reached the porch steps and I feared/hoped she might come right up and invite herself in for dinner, she angled her body slightly to veer around the steps, skirting the edge of the porch as if someone had just plunked this house down in her path where she would normally have kept on.

When she was within a few feet of where I stood, barely breathing, she slowed, slightly. Raised her head, barely. And sniffed. Then, continued on, around the porch and to the far side of the cabin where she disappeared from view on route to the creek. She didn't see me. I may as well have been part of the house, an obstacle in her way.

A year had passed since the three bears first took over the apple tree. They had seemed so comfortable, so content munching in the grass by the driveway that I was surprised when, after gobbling the last apple, they packed up and left. I didn't see so much as a track in the interim. Which was for the best, I guess, considering all the dangers of humans, all the neighbors with guns at the ready and shooting year-round.

I still hadn't seen one deer. Not one, though their tracks abounded in the forest mud, or by the creek, where they must have come down at night. It's a strange paradox to see more deer in suburban towns and even cities, like Missoula Montana where a buck hung out in my sister's tiny "fenced" yard for a week, nibbling her nasturtiums. Here, their absence year-round suggested to me that some of my neighbors might not abide by hunting seasons. Or maybe it was just the continual shooting, at any hour, in all weather, any time of year, like a never-ending fourth of July, stressful to me but potentially deadly to my wild neighbors.

So, I didn't blame them for staying away. I had my own No Trespassing signs at the start of my driveway in an attempt to keep uninvited human visitors out. If only I could post signs at the edge of the forest welcoming the wild visitors in. You're safe *here*, I wanted to tell them. But I couldn't speak for my human neighbors. The ones with the Trump banners and guns, I didn't feel safe around either. Probably, like me and the deer, they were just scared. But as gun-toting white men supporting a fascist dictator-wannabe, the power dynamic was decidedly different.

It was a relief, then, to come home one afternoon in my second October of residence and round the corner by the apple tree to see a large chestnut-brown rump retreating into the forest. That night, and a week of nights to follow, I heard crunching, shifting branches, slight cracking sounds, and more apple munching. Lying in bed, I listened, smiling in the darkness.

No cubs that year, and the one I assumed was Momma Bear seemed especially shy and skittish on her own, easily spooked back into the forest at the slightest human sound, even the click of my front door opening. So, I tried my best to stay out of her way, stay out of the woods for a while so as not to scare her farther in with my scent.

That weekend, sunny and still, I looked out the window to see her there. She'd stand up, reach up with her front paws—opposable thumbs not required—pull branches down to grab an apple, then plop down in the grass and chew. Arms splayed in front of her, like a plush toy. Stand up, grab an apple, plop down and munch. And again, and again.

I pulled a chair to the window and watched, wanting to stretch time, willing her to stay. Knowing, now, that she'd be gone again once she'd finished the apples.

A few times she paused, sniffing, or listening to neighbors' weekend goings-on, then continued her feasting. It was an honor just to witness her, an honor to give her the space she needed to enjoy her apples, to head into winter that much more prepared. Even if she never saw me. Probably, though, she knew I was there. I ate three apples that year, left the rest for her.

The squirrels see me—watch me, even. Of course they do; I put out food. They care not one whit whether I call it "bird food." After an epic six-month squirrel battle which involved multiple feeder locations, various barricades, and switching out the types of feeders (you'd think I would have it down by now, but I believe squirrels may be getting smarter), I finally found the right setup such that the bird feeders were left to the birds and the squirrels were welcome—and encouraged—to clean up below. Though, because I'm a softie, I do also toss out cracked corn and peanuts just for them.

The larger, bolder, suburbanite gray squirrels moved on once they couldn't empty the seed feeders anymore, but the Douglas squirrels remained. Douglas squirrels, named for the Douglas fir cones they specialize in, would be here under the fir canopy whether there were additional sunflower seeds/peanuts/cracked corn to forage or not. They're cheerful little chaps, barely larger than chipmunks with auburn fur and dark puppydog eyes. And like puppies, mostly they explore and play and eat and tussle, and vocalize like tiny toy ray guns at anything that surprises or frightens them. Which is everything.

I have a difficult time determining the number of individuals who reside in the yard as they're difficult to tell apart, but I estimate there might be two or three adults whose overlapping territories include my back porch feeder area, give or take three to eight juveniles who might be tagging along learning the ropes before their parents kick them out to find their own territories. Now that they are used to me, my movements and routines and peanut-tossing, they all generally go about their business, aware of me, it is clear, but unalarmed. I can sit on my back porch or against the Douglas fir just beyond and enjoy their antics, watch them chase each other, corkscrewing up one fir and down the next, chattering all the while. Squirrel TV is one of my favorite shows.

One spring, though, I noticed an individual Douglas squirrel. I noticed her because part of her right ear was missing. Torn, or bitten—she'd had a rough time of it, somehow, and my heart opened to her more than the others. I looked for her and made sure to toss peanuts near her. I spoke to her, addressed her directly. I saw her.

Focusing in on that one squirrel, I noticed her extended belly, noticed her waddle as she moved around the yard. Noticed eight sets of swollen nipples. And sure enough, several weeks later, I watched as she paraded four miniature versions of her from tree to tree. Late summer, nearly fall, she had another litter, another parade of awkward squeaking tussling tots at her heels. I was impressed; that's no small feat in a forest with ravens and weasels and owls and eagles and coyotes and bobcats and others who would fancy baby squirrel for dinner. That raggedy-eared female squirrel—she was tough. Just watching her made me happy.

That fall, as the rains came and I spent less time in the yard and more time on the covered back porch, it became clear that the one squirrel I'd been watching was also watching me. Whether I was sitting with my coffee tuning in to the sights and sounds of the yard, or wrapped in a blanket tapping away on my laptop or distracted by my phone, sooner or later, Raggedy Ear would come bounding across the yard from the garage, or descend from one of the firs, or just suddenly appear on the ground in front of me. But unlike the other squirrels who would go about their business when I was around—an honor in itself to be dismissed as no threat—that one Douglas squirrel would, inevitably, come up on to the porch, right up to my feet, and look up at me. Not just generally in my direction, but directly in my face—her eyes seeking mine, animal to animal. She saw me.

Just begging, you say, just asking for a peanut like a domesticated pet? Perhaps. Except she wasn't a pet. As comfortable as she seemed around me, she remained a wild animal. A furred beastlet who could fit in the palm of my hand, who I could have crushed under my boot. A prey animal who slept out every night all year in a leafy nest in grandmother cedar, or one of the firs, or tunneled in a rotting stump, in torrential rains, heavy snows, and searing heat. Who spent her days foraging and feasting sixty feet up in the canopy, on the forest floor, or on the stump under the overhang of my garage. An individual who made a hundred choices every day, doing her best to take care of herself, to stay alive in our shared home. That one of her choices was to seek out a giant bumbling human, to come close, to say with her big brown eyes, *please?* That's not nothing.

Yes, I said. *Here's a peanut*, I said. *You're safe with me*, I told her. *Thank you*, I meant. Thank you.

Steller's jays love peanuts too. They care not one whit whether I call it "squirrel food." They too quickly learned my habits, know I typically toss out corn and peanuts in the morning. In the murky pre-dawn light when I open the door to the back porch, I see their punk rock silhouettes in the low branches of the young hemlock tree. Two or three of them, usually, maybe silently waiting, maybe chortling amongst themselves in anticipation. They see me.

It's you! They say. *It's you!* I say. *Thank you,* we say. I toss out peanuts.

Chickadees, too, would reside in the area whether I supplemented their food or not. But with sunflower seeds in steady supply, they've formed aerial superhighways where on most dry days I might see both the Oreo-striped black-capped and russet-tinged chestnut-backed chickadees zipping to and from the balcony feeders on routes so regular I could map them.

One afternoon I was pruning some dead branches from a young cedar tree when a chestnut-backed chickadee paused on her journey, landing in that tree, a few branches above. I paused in my work and looked up at her. Instead of zooming on as I expected she'd do—chickadees never seem to stay still for very long—she hopped down closer to me. A bird the size of a walnut stood on toothpick legs a mere foot from my face, tilted her head sideways and focused one shining coal-black eye on mine.

She held my gaze for three, long, seconds.

Then with a brief *chip* she sprung back into motion and rejoined the others. I stood there, mouth agape, basking in the intimacy of our meeting.

Another afternoon, in the backyard halfway to the creek, I squatted down to check out a mushroom. I'd only been able to identify three of the maybe dozens of species that might pop up at any time of year, so I mostly noticed and attempted to distinguish them, without knowing their names. This one was a generic sort of beige mushroom with a straight stalk and plain cap, the kind of mushroom a child (or I) might draw, a mushroomy mushroom.

I was fully engrossed in trying to find some identifying characteristic that might help me as I leafed through my field guides later, when I heard the whoosh of heavy wings above me. Still squatting, I looked up to see a bald eagle had landed in one of the spindly alders above the creekbank, above me. The tree bowed and swayed under her weight but she countershifted her head to keep it steady, her piercing gaze on me.

I felt small. Vulnerable, even, though she was no threat to me. Something about her size, her position above, my crouched position below, and especially, those eyes on me, chastened me. I was catapulted back down the line to my ancestors, back to when we were all, always, immersed in our landscapes, prey and predator, in intimate relationship with the more-than-human world.

Maybe she wasn't as interested in me personally as whether I might be coveting something of actual interest to her—like a fish. Or maybe she was just curious about this crouching animal. And, maybe the reasoning didn't matter so much as the simple fact that I met an eagle that day, and she met me. I held my place below her, a disciple kneeling before her, and I held her eyes. As the alder stilled, she stilled, and held my eyes. We witnessed each other.

Another raptor sought me out, one evening. I'd heard the jays and robins making a ruckus about something, and I've learned that a twilight ruckus often means an owl is awake and on the move. I went out to sit against Grandmother cedar, at the spot where I'd placed some trimmed boughs from a young cedar to made a comfortable sitting spot between two buttressed roots even more comfortable, and I waited.

Most times I hear this sort of fussing and squawking and go out seeking the source, I find nothing but agitated robins and jays. Every once in a while, with the aid of binoculars and the patience to wait them out, I might spot an owl flying away.

This night was different. I just sat, and listened, and let my gaze soften, unfocus. I relaxed my head back against the red-brown bark. And then, the owl came to me. Soaring silently across the driveway out of the forest, with a trail of squawking songbirds, she landed in the cedar directly above me and looked down. I looked up.

Barred owl. Dark stripes on buff body, smooth round head and giant eyes like two eclipsed suns, pointed at me.

I'd seen and even been seen by barred owls before, more often, I think, than any other wild animals I've encountered in my wanders around the country. I recall a meeting in the sultry swamps of Florida, an owl perched in a cypress in the murky mosquitoed afternoon light. Another in a New Hampshire woodland, high in the one red oak in a birch and maple grove, red and yellow leaves swirling around. And still another on the mossy threshold of a nest cavity in a moss and fern-draped bigleaf maple tree dripping with Oregon rain.

Meeting this species again, this individual for the first time in my new home, felt good. It felt right. The sort of neighbor that makes a house even more a home. To witness and be witnessed by this wild neighbor, to see and be seen, it mattered.

It matters.

Why does it matter? I've long felt that the natural world is not a scenic backdrop for human activity. That to immerse myself in the natural world is to be among a rich community of fascinating and endearing individuals. The closer I look, the more individuals I see. And, truly seeing, I ache to know.

In this home we share, I long to reach across the divide that separates all of us and try to be a good neighbor, a kind neighbor. One who makes wild ones feel welcome, and, perhaps, sometimes, want to reach back. And maybe, let me know I'm welcome too.

I'm still human, and I understand if wild animals don't want to reach back, ever. Not feeling safe with my kind, because of all we've done and continue to do. I get that. My own No Trespassing signs aimed at strangers I don't know and certain neighbors I know enough to worry they might be dangerous, are much the same.

But those signs? They aren't just about me, and my safety. I aim to protect the wild residents too, the ones who were here first and whose descendants will hopefully be here long after. In my actions, my way of interacting with and being on the land, I aim to be a gentle caretaker, a conscientious roommate. Even if I never saw a single wild animal; it just feels like the right thing to do.

The fact that I do see some of them is a gift. To watch, to recognize, to get to know. In those rare times when an individual comes in close, reaching across the divide to see me back, for brief moments, I am no longer a solitary hermit hiding from real life. I am just one of many animals, a good neighbor, at home in my village.

6

Spinster

Dear 17-year-old self,

I know you're going through a rough time—your first love has ended in your first heartbreak. He just didn't want you anymore, and now you wonder how you will ever get past this. Don't worry, I'm not going to tell you that you're just young, or that you're overreacting, or that you don't know what real heartbreak feels like—because that's bullshit. This is it. That wrenching pain in your chest, that hollow feeling in your stomach—it comes from knowing deep intimacy, from mutual adoration with another human who holds you close, looks you in the eyes, and makes you feel so alive, so important, so safe. That's the strongest drug in the world, and when you lose it, it will fucking hurt. You will suffer, and that's as real as it gets. I'm sorry to say, it will feel the same every single time.

You don't want to hear that. And you most certainly don't want to hear that thirty years from now, you won't be married or even partnered. You will have been single for so long that you've almost forgotten what that drug feels like—but not quite. Every few years, you'll dabble in love and loss and find that neither they nor you have changed much in that arena. I know you're terrified of ending up alone and though neither of us knows yet about the "ending up" part, at least in middle age, yes, you will be very much alone.

Hear me out. That pain? That broken feeling? That's not what alone feels like. That has nothing to do with alone. That is only and always about withdrawal from the love drug. And that drug, let me tell you, it makes you stupid. Every time. Every time, you put everything into it, give yourself over completely to all that they are and that you are together until you lose your self. Like addicts everywhere, you can't handle just a little, always need more, your next fix—their attention, their gaze, their touch—until it consumes you. Every. Single. Time. At least so far.

You may notice I've been vague with the pronouns. Why not just say he/him/his? Why not discuss the husband you won't have? Because in thirty years, you also won't have a wife, though you could—it's legal now. And here's newsflash number two: you're not straight. Deep down you know that already, though you won't realize it for another three years or so when college life finally breaks through your sheltered suburban socialization.

Remember seventh grade? Remember Jody? The way your whole body ignited when she was around, showing off in gym class or clowning around in the lockered hallways? How each time those ice-blue eyes locked on yours, you felt the most curious sort of warmth gushing into your nether regions? How you managed to become her shy fawning friend for a while, passing notes in the hallway, exchanging small gifts like sticks of Juicyfruit gum or vending machine jewelry and it was all going so well and you were so very happy in a way you'd never been before and couldn't explain to your regular friends, until everything changed. As it does. As it must, one way or another, or we'd all die of adrenalated ardor poisoning.

True, that one changed more abruptly than most—more abruptly than any that would come later. Later you'll realize she must have caught on, consciously or not, to what was really going on, and she wasn't ready to face it any more than you were and the only way she knew how to deal with it in her tough-girl tomboy probably future-butch baby-dyke or who knows maybe actually totally straight way was to catch your eye in social studies and mouth the words *Fuck You* which struck as a blade in your chest and then she never looked at you again, you may has well have been a ghost, invisible, gone.

So, you see? This first love you are pining now? He wasn't the first. She was. It doesn't matter that she was a girl and you didn't understand what was going on and you were only thirteen. You've been here before. Is it any easier this time now that you're older and wiser? No. Of course not.

But that won't stop you from trying. You'll stick with boys though college, then you'll dabble with girls until you go full-on lesbian in your twenties—all of it. The spiky hair, rainbow jewelry and bumper stickers, gay bars and pride parades, emotionally and sexually-charged incestuous friend circles worthy of your own *L-Word* television series, long before that show appears on Showtime.

Eventually, you'll date a man again, and then a woman, and then both at the same time, and you'll decide you weren't a lesbian after all, and for a while you'll use the label bisexual and eventually settle on queer when you realize that for you, romantic and sexual attraction has nothing to do with body parts or gender identification and everything to do with who a person is aside from all that, and if you think that might make things simpler, it won't.

Whether they are woman, man, or non-binary, whoever they are with you or who you are together, you will try to be both lover and loved. You'll try because you can't help it, feel some primal compulsion to seek out and connect physically and emotionally intimately with an other of your species, despite how it makes you act, despite how you fear it will turn out.

The physical part, at least, you understand. The endorphin-charged urge to mate, to copulate and consummate regardless of whether you'll procreate. If you could separate out the physical part, enjoy it for what it is—like you enjoy an artisan, hand-tossed, heirloom tomato, garden-fresh basil pizza with a glass of cabernet sauvignon—you'd be so much better off. (Yes, thirty years later, pizza is still your favorite food. You'll just dress it up classier and accompany it with wine or beer like a grown-up. But of course, yes, it's still pizza, and you'll still consider pizza the most perfect food.) Some can separate sex from emotional intimacy. Or maybe they just pretend to? Not you, so don't bother.

You will have good sex. Plenty of it, don't you worry. But, whether in your handful of long-ish committed relationships or what will look more like one-night stands, you'll always get attached—consumed, addicted. Not to the physical act alone, but to the whole messy confusing fascinating beautiful vulnerable authentic human you shared it with.

What you'll come to realize, much later, is that the power of romantic intimacy lies in the fact that through some fault of your biochemical makeup and the intensity, the depth of that intimacy, that other person so quickly comes to feel like an extension of yourself, a part of who you are, so that you can only feel right and content and whole when you are with them. Such that the lack of them creates a hole, an amputation, a death of your self. You're feeling this now; you know what I mean. The writers of all those sappy, syrupy, crooning love songs know it too. Something about love turns us all back into groveling, mawkish teenagers. No offense.

So. If that part won't get easier, if you won't be any better at love and loss thirty years from now, where does that leave us?

Well, currently, pushing fifty and alone. Even if fifty is the new thirty or whatever the saying is these days, there's no denying I'm firmly into spinster territory now. Not the respectable unmarried professional spinning woman of 1500s Europe, but also not the shameful sinful unmarried woman failing to fulfill her God-decreed duty to serve man as wife and mother. Who is the spinster of post-millennial secular America? Mostly, in my experience, we are invisible. And, as such, we are left to define ourselves, for ourselves.

And here's my point. Remember what I said about being alone? Before I went and distracted you with lesbians, pizza, and love songs? Just this: alone and heartbreak are two very different things. All those amputated broken empty feelings are simply withdrawal symptoms. They may not get any easier, but they don't last. They go away, and then you are left to rebuild your self, on your own. And that, my young self, does get easier.

With each loss and each stretch of aloneness, you grow more confidently, contentedly, even lovingly into who you really are and who you are becoming. Toward the older, wiser woman you aim to be. You learn to take care of yourself, not look to anyone else to do it for you. You get better and better at it, because you take the time to listen, to attend to what nourishes you, what pleasures and delights and comforts you on the deepest levels. Eventually, finally, you come to know, not just intellectually but in the deepest fibers of your animal body, that you are whole, that you have always been whole, and truly, honestly, genuinely don't need anybody else. Not in that petulant stubborn independence of a child insistent on making her own way, but in the calm, exhilarating freedom of a middle-aged woman who's released the shackles of a tired cultural norm and finally walked out into the sunlight, positively bursting with ardor for all the lovers who came before, for all the messy confusing fascinating beautiful vulnerable authentic human connections out there, but also for the more-than-human world, for your home and landscape and your aging body and love itself.

That, dear one, is what alone can feel like. That is the kind of spinster you will be one day, but only, first, if you pick yourself up and get back out there.

7

Hermit

The rain returned. Clean water fell from the sky, rinsing smoke and ash from the conifers, my sloped roof, the yellowing vine maples, the evergreen ferns, and the orange hawkweed flowers gone to seed, all filtering down to the creek and out to the rivers to the sea. I listened in the darkness, giddy with gratitude and relief.

I woke up smiling, ran around the house opening windows and doors to release the stagnant air, then ran outside, releasing myself.

I could breathe again. For a few days, I'd be acutely aware of how precious that gift is—a pure, hedonistic joy just to fill my lungs with clean, fresh air. There were other places, within a half-day's drive, where that was not the case. I don't mean polluted, treeless cities—that's old news—but dense forests like this one. Woodland hideaways just like mine.

The previous day, and the ten days before that, the sky glowed sickly yellow, the sun blazed a radioactive red, and the tops of the trees were shrouded in thick smog. Standing for brief moments in my gravel driveway, looking up, it was confusing, incongruous, a post-apocalyptic movie or a nightmare with the set all wrong. That inert sky and toxic air belonged in the unregulated industrial zones of a developing nation, or Los Angeles, or at least the arid wildfire-ready landscapes east of the Cascades mountains through the Rocky Mountain foothills. Not here. Not the moss-carpeted fern-lush cedar fir rainforests of the Pacific Northwest. Not after one of the wettest winters on record with heavy rains into June so that locals joked about "Juneuary." Why, come September, were Washington and Oregon burning? It doesn't make sense.

It does make sense. I know the science. Decades of fire suppression plus the perfect fusion of late summer heat, lightning, high winds, a dash of human recklessness in some cases, and, of course, the key factor amplifying natural disasters everywhere: human-caused climate change. Erratic and catastrophic: the new normal. Hurricanes cycling through multiple alphabets in the southeast, the same. Tornados touching down where they hadn't before, tsunamis and tidal waves the same. Turn on the news or any weather report and you'll hear phrases like "most/highest/worst _____ on record" and descriptors like "unprecedented" so often they've lost their meaning.

When my Montana-dwelling sister used to complain about another wildfire season, of her smoke alarm going off inside despite all windows shut tight, I felt a sort of self-righteous pity. When a childhood friend residing in Florida was evacuated for the third time in one year in advance of the latest hurricane, I felt the same. Sorry, but aren't you asking for that, living there? Why not, if you have the mobility, choose to live somewhere safer?

A brazenly privileged point of view. But also, increasingly irrelevant. There is, now, nowhere safer. Rainforests are burning. So far, my home hasn't been in immediate danger. But it could have been. One of these years, it will be.

Those ten days, my wild sanctuary felt like a prison. In the warmth of a sunny September when I should have had the windows open to fresh breezes wafting ripening apples, when I should have enjoyed lazy, mosquito-free afternoons on the porch, in the hammock, or reading by the creek, I was instead shut inside in the fusty air, face pressed to the glass, eyeing the orange sun. Everywhere within a day's drive, the air quality spanned from hazardous to off the charts, the worst in the world, they said.

Finally, I could breathe again—outside, and free.

I'd always dreamed of a covered porch, to be outside and sheltered from the elements. If this home didn't come with one I'd have built one eventually, something humble, something basic like this. A platform balcony off the slant-rooved bedroom above shelters ten two-by-fours nailed together and balanced on cinder blocks, room enough for a comfy chair and small end table out of the rain. On weekend mornings, I wrap up in a wool blanket and sit out with my coffee, surrounded by my gregarious neighbors—the Steller's jays and Douglas squirrels—to whom I toss peanuts and cracked corn.

That post-apocalyptic smoke-free morning on my backyard perch, coffee steaming on the coaster, rain dripping from the hemlocks and cedars, neighbors chattering and tussling over breakfast, the rushing sound of the creek rising from down the hill, rain mist on my face redolent with sweet cedar perfume, all was right with the world again.

Except it wasn't. Did I mention we were in the height of the Covid-19 pandemic? That I couldn't gather with human friends even if I wanted to, nor safely travel to visit my family, that masks and hand sanitizer and handwashing and social distancing were the new normal among human animals? That staff meetings and literary readings and happy hours and concerts and workshops were all virtual, all video, all flat, 2-D experiences to consume from a glowing screen?

Did I mention the police violence and social unrest? The racial justice protests and counterprotests turning to riots in the cities—my city, not far from here? Did I mention that many to most of my country neighbors professed to love the fascist president who fanned those flames, other straight white men who love their guns and their freedom and their country which is only their country because our ancestors stole it, their idea of freedom an elitist privilege built on genocide, slavery, and hypocrisy? That the American greatness they are willing to fight for with their bullets and teargas appears to me as nothing more than straight male white power?

Sometimes, I can't breathe. Even when the air is clear, when I'm home in my private little hermitage at the end of the road—a relatively safe place, protected, so far, from most of the horrors out there in the real world. And I still, sometimes, can't breathe.

Maybe it's the hormones, a hot flash coming on. Maybe it's the plague, Covid coming on. Or maybe my idea of separateness, of safety and oblivion in my hideout is an illusion. Like the yellow smoke, the chemical toxins wafting in on the wind from far off lands biochemically urging me to flee though there's nowhere within a day's drive to flee to and what's out there will reach me anyway. You can hide, but you can't run.

As a single, solitary, introverted nature nerd, my various wildland abodes have served as retreats—refuges where I could shut out the strife of the human world, release the static, the stress, the nonsensical importance of the daily grind and plug back in to the real world, the natural world. But the real world is on fire. The toxic ash of old growth trees, burned buildings, animals, and human animals may no longer be seeping into my windows, burning my eyes, constricting my throat, and filling my heart with a panicked anxiety that says go, now, when there's nowhere to go. The fires are still out there. Physical, and cultural fires. Our whole species, it seems, is self-destructing, conflagrating, imploding, and dragging the earth down with us.

I will join the resistance, fight the good fight. Get out there among my own kind, physically or virtually, speak out, talk back, use my own privilege to stand up for human justice and earth justice. I will.

I should.
I haven't.

There have always been hermits. Sanctified and justified when associated with mainstream religions: monks, nuns, anchorites, eremites, ascetics... or, chastised and feared when not associated with the in-group: witches, recluses, loners, madmen, crazy cat ladies.

Whatever you call us, however we are accepted or not, what are we really doing out here in our caves/deserts/cells/cabins/woodlands? Do we set ourselves apart because we're tapping in to something real, remembering something bigger than ourselves and our self-absorbed species, trying to live on a higher plane? Or, are we all just maladapted antisocial cowards with the privilege and means to hide?

Could both be true?

From each sword fern island in my yard, a frog croaked. An Anna's hummingbird I hadn't seen for weeks hummed up to my coffee mug, then over to the newly filled nectar feeder hanging from the balcony. As the rain let up the chickadees resumed their chittering forays from balcony feeder to fir and back again. A Douglas squirrel, after finding no more peanuts, toddled up to my foot and looked up at me with searching brown eyes that melt my heart in ways that human babies are supposed to but never have.

I think I will stay here, breathing among them, a while longer.

8

Hag

I hadn't bled in five months. Each time it happened, I wondered: *Am I done? Was that it? Have I finally crossed the threshold into the 'after,' whatever that might mean?*

So far, the answer was no. I found that I was, and had been for five years and counting, in the in-between time. Neither mother—still possible but unlikely—nor crone, not yet. And like that liminal space between maiden and mother, girl and woman—I was continually, incessantly, trying to determine who I was and what on earth was happening with my body.

Nobody sits you down and gives you the 'becoming a crone' talk, even those of us lucky enough to have had the 'becoming a woman' talk from a scientifically-informed and minimally awkward mother, complemented with biologically accurate, judgement-free human physiology and sex ed. in school. Underneath all that awkwardness, the anxiety around dealing with the changes of puberty and cultural norms on keeping our monthly bleeds and hormonal upheavals secret or only confided among girlfriends, underneath the unspoken shame was also a certain pride. A badge of honor in becoming a woman. A woman, i.e., a potential mother. Same same.

So, at forty-three, when I first started experiencing signs of another change—biologically inevitable, though a bit early—I didn't recognize it. Didn't understand that certain symptoms might be connected, might have more to do with internal hormonal upheaval than the various external causes I sought and sometimes failed to identify. Unexplained weight gain, hypersensitive, rashy skin, and increasingly intense, erratic mood swings akin to PMS symptoms, but at any time. All the time.

A couple years later when a female doctor learned of my erratic periods and finally said the word perimenopause, I was told only that I should eat less and exercise more. *Congratulations, you're in the process of 'un-becoming.'*

I understand that for many women, this was the part where we might grow wistful at losing the capacity to grow a new life. Beyond the cultural significance, the expectations and norms of motherhood, there is something real, something powerful in marking that transition out of it, of losing that superpower, that creative force that no man will ever have and in my opinion is the root of all misogyny, all patriarchy, the original inferiority complex that incited/incites men to wield their muscle mass to dominate us, to swear by and kill for a holy father/son creator, to compensate for the fact that every one of them was formed by and born out of a woman's body. Meaning, I do recognize that motherhood is a big deal.

And yet, for a variety of reasons, not all women possess or use that superpower. I will never know what it is like to grow another human inside my own body, to bring that human into the world, watch her grow and care for her like an extension of my self. Unlike some women, I also have no misgivings or regrets about that. I truly believe that motherhood wasn't my path in this life. That I wouldn't have been a good mother, not the kind I would have wanted to be, and that choosing not to bring another human into this world was the best choice not just for me, but for that child.

So, while I am in awe of and grateful for my potential capacity to mother, I did not mourn that physiology as it slipped away. Maybe that's why it was going so early: use it or lose it.

As for the physical changes, I've never felt beautiful in that media-reinforced Caucasian American ideal of porcelain-skinned doll-like face, skinny girlish body with padding permissible only around the mothering parts— breasts and a hint of mothering hips. My muscled, sturdy girl body grew into a burly, husky adult body collecting pounds and scars by the year. So, unlike some women in midlife just beginning to lose the male—or female—gaze, I also didn't mourn some recent loss of attractiveness; that ship had sailed.

And finally, I hadn't suddenly become aware of my mortality as I've heard the change can trigger, having been an introspective brooder since my introspective brooding teenage years, always perfectly aware that this life is finite and I am going to die. Based on my physical health and family history, I could either live well into my nineties, only halfway there, or die unexpectedly of aggressive cancer any day now. In either case, there's not much to be done about it.

So, then, chugging along toward menopause should have been easy, right? Should have been a relief, even. Why bring this up at all?

Because outside of all those socially constructed roles and judgements, outside of who I was or was becoming to anyone else, I found my own, intimate self feeling more than ever unstable. Physically, emotionally, mentally, all of who made me, me, felt increasingly precarious.

As adolescents that wasn't quite so strange, because we hadn't had so long to get used to anything; as children, we were always growing, always changing. Our families, schools, and society made us constantly aware of that in all the age/height/grade level benchmarks we aimed always to surpass. Puberty was just a magnification of those changes, the final push into adulthood, where we would be done growing, fully formed humans. Any turmoil after that was simply situational, external, existential. Once I'd reached adulthood, I occasionally sensed a growing feeling of equanimity in my self, a comfortable familiarity despite whatever might have been going on in the world around me. I expected that would deepen as I aged, the turmoil fading completely. It didn't. Quite the opposite.

Who was I, and what on earth was going on with my body?

I was on fire. Hot flashes, crimson flushes, and night sweats surged through my body at random intervals. That only occasionally visible sign of perimenopause and the only part addressed in jest on television and movies but generally hidden or ignored in real life was more complex, more bizarre, and more intense than I'd ever imagined. Ten second burning fevers, brief personal dry saunas, or sometimes, sweat lodges. Inconsistent and changeable for years, so that I could never predict, never know when or how the next one would arrive.

One month they came on multiple times an hour, all day long. Another month I couldn't stop sweating, dripping puddles on my yoga mat like a teenage boy lifting weights, and all I was doing was warrior pose. Sometimes they seemed to emanate from my core, around my heart, but more often I could feel my face burn first, then my ears, then it crept down my neck until I knew if I looked in the mirror I would appear as a freshly seared lobster. A later addition to my repertoire was chills—cold flashes?—that were equally intense and confusing and when combined with the hot flashes had me putting on and throwing off sweaters and blankets so often it might have been comical if anyone else was around to notice, which they generally were not.

Sometimes they were preceded by a sudden pang of dread, as if death herself was hovering, hot breath on my cheek, considering whether to take me. Other times they were accompanied by a sudden Zen-like calm, as if transported to my own private beach on a hot summer day and I could almost hear the waves. Rather than an out-of-body experience, hot flashes are uniquely in-body, drawing me instantly back, entirely in, briefly aware of nothing else but myself, alone and on fire.

I'd always had a lot of internal fire as they say in naturopathy or traditional Chinese medicine, and my pale skin had always been prone to blushing. But I know now that a youthful blush is as similar to a perimenopausal hot flash as a lizard is to T-Rex. My internal furnace was not ticking away anymore, it was utterly on the fritz, blazing out of control, starting and stalling out like a tired engine, heading toward burnout.

And then, what? I didn't know. Perhaps I'd just be cold.

Also, I was awake. *Hello, darkness, my old friend.* Hello, 3 a.m., again. I had never used to have trouble sleeping, no matter what was going on with me. Sure, sometimes, busy-brain obsessing kept me from falling asleep for a spell, eating or drinking too late could wake me in the night, leave me tossing and turning for a while, but never this. Never, full on, give up and turn on the light and read or maybe even get up go outside and stargaze for a while because it was going to be another long night with capital I Insomnia.

If I could have adjusted the rest of my life to my body's unpredictable schedule, it wouldn't have been so bad. Sleep for a few hours every evening, wake in the night, then nap again late morning, afternoon too. Live like a housecat. That sounded nice. Maybe, one day long in the future when I could actually afford to retire, I would get to try that.

Locked in to the 8 – 4 job that cared not whether I'd had a wink of sleep the night before, my body and mind were at odds. Literally out of sync, and short of succumbing to the slippery slope of sleeping pills, there didn't seem to be a single thing I could do about it. Awake—sweating, shivering, sweating—and blinking in the darkness.

I was crawling out of my skin. My skin, dry and scaly despite twice or thrice daily lotions, creams, and salves. My skin, itchy and reactive, rashing up under my waistband, bra strap, glasses on my ears. Rashing from sunshine, from seasonal allergies, from too much junk food, from an unrealistic workload at the day job, the state of the union, the fascist ex-president, the fascist ex-president's followers, from something inside of me itching to get out. I scratched my skin, the visible rash, but the itch went deeper.

I cleaned, everything. Dusted, vacuumed, swept, polished, and scrubbed until it shined. I organized and reorganized my house, my garage, my office, my life. I bought things—stocked the cupboards with food, hit the thrift stores for more clothes, dishes, knick-knacks. I planted things, pulled weeds, trimmed shrubs, arranged and rearranged the lawn chairs. Sometimes I even went jogging. And though I scratched, the itch remained.

Sometimes, I was animal in rut. Wet and ready like a teenager. Like when I was a teenager, with the teenage boys who were right there with me ready to tear off our clothes and hump like rabbits. But there weren't any men now. Or women.

When I used to teach adolescents, I would joke that they had hormone poisoning. Everyone knows this about adolescents. They don't tell you about this other time, when hormonal shifts cause the same sort of drives but stronger, with adult longings and know-how. I think if I actually had someone in front of me lusting back, I might have torn them apart, devoured them like a praying mantis and licked my lips afterward.

Other times, I was inert, my body and its urges dried up completely. A preview of what was to come, when I finally crossed over? Which was equal parts sad—all that ferocious desire gone to waste—and a relief.

I was, often, angry. The fledgling wrath of a teenage girl matured into the rage of a middle-aged woman with nothing to lose. No longer dependent daughter, nobody's wife, nobody's mother. A whirling dervish with no restraints. One month I lashed out at a neighbor whose dog came into my yard, barely, once. I'd become *that* neighbor.

I never knew what might unleash the beast—callousness, injustice, misunderstanding, apathy, confusion, clumsiness, stubbed toe, spilled milk, no external cause whatsoever and I was suddenly instantly consumed by a searing white-hot fury, a mental hot flash capable of emotional and potentially even physical violence to anyone who dared stand in my way. No socially-accepted mama bear protecting her cubs, I was, instead, a solitary, stark-raving wolverine. And if you came too close at the wrong time, I would slash you.

Some studies suggest that estrogen is an aggression-dampening hormone, which, in consort with other estrogen-regulated hormones like serotonin, makes us docile, more likely to roll over and expose our necks to the males of our species, to be agreeable mates, gentle mothers, level-headed matriarchs. And then, no longer in need of that softness, of that submissiveness, we shed it like tired old skins.

So maybe, I was not broken. Maybe, this was who I really was, free of my shackles.

I was hungry. Or maybe I was not actually hungry in terms of needing vitamins, minerals and calories—long done growing and soon to be shrinking—but a deep desirous yearning demanded... something. I wanted. I craved. I salivated for some thing to satiate my corporeal desire. Food was what I could get my hands on, my mouth on, to swirl around on my tongue, to chew and swallow and fill at least my belly, for a while. A hot cup of coffee and warm cinnamon scone from the local bakery. Basil pesto tortellini salad with cherry tomatoes from the local farmer's market. Creamy vanilla ice cream swirled with tart red huckleberries picked fresh from the yard. Honey-balsamic roast duck from a friend's farm that I gave up attempting to carve and picked up whole with my bare hands and tore into with my teeth, juices dripping down my wrists.

I was crying—again. It didn't feel like sadness or depression. Not that gauzy slow darkness that descends on others I know. My tears simply a sprung leak, all that emotion bottled and swirling—burning/anxious/exhausted/itchy/lusting/furious/ravenous—never fully expressed, never fully satisfied, seeping salty hot rivulets down my scarlet cheeks. Emotional overwhelm distilled to pure grief. For all the hateful heartless apathetic humans, all the harm we continue to cause to each other and the more-than-human world. When all the other emotions were spent and all that's left was clear, crystalline mourning for what was and what could be.

It didn't last long. I felt too alive, too full of wonder, delight, and gratitude for this miraculous life on this beautiful planet. And that I got to live, for a while, in my own feral little corner of it among ancient trees, a cheerful creek, comical squirrels, fascinating birds, vibrant wildflowers, tart berry bushes, cleansing rains, and on and on ad infinitum and though I realized we are all connected to everything else, all the good and bad going on out there in the greater world, and how precarious it all is and is becoming more so as we bring on the havoc of climate change, right then, right there, in that woodland at the end of the gravel road, in relationship primarily with myself and the land, I was fiercely alive, and intended to remain so for a long, long time. I may have been losing the capacity to create new life, but I planned to fully inhabit this one.

So, let's just put it out there: I was—am—a witch. Not by the modern definition— no prescribed rituals, no spells involved— but in the original sense of the word. I think, perhaps, that I had been becoming her my whole life, and have only recently arrived. Collecting wrinkles, scars, unsightly folds of skin. Barefoot and wild-haired, red-faced and unapologetically ranting, raving, emoting. Immersed in the natural world, friends with animals, making medicines of plants, self-sufficient and content, on my own. Most assuredly without need of male company or assistance. And, society tells me, no longer of any use to men. Possibly, someone to pity or even fear. The unapologetic, archetypal witch.

My male ancestors slaughtered more than nine million women over five generations just for being as I am. Once upon a time, they would have burned me too. Maybe they still will.

Or, try to medicate me. But I don't want hormones to mollify me, to keep me wet and ready, to stave off the inevitable. I'm done trying to grow into the woman society said I should be, giving in to metamorphosing into the human animal, the witch, the hag I really am.

I hadn't bled in six months. Heavy cramping, deep scarlet blood, big chunky clots. Almost as if I was miscarrying something, the final push to clear out what no longer served me. It lasted nearly three weeks. I wanted to think of it as the big finale. Clearing the way, cleaning out the cobwebs, opening the portal. The way forward, the way home. But more likely, I wasn't done yet. How do you recognize and mark the passage, that milestone, when you can't clearly identify it?

9

Cat Lady

A year into my solitary cabin life, I remained catless. *Between cats*, I used to say, but after ten years without one, I had to face the fact that I was just—catless. Which was surprising; I had thought I would have had a mess of cats by then. A clowder, according to most collective noun lists, though I much prefer the alternate name: glaring. A clowder, etymologically, is a clutter, another word for a mess, which could be true for any group of animals and doesn't tell you much of anything about cats. Most cats I've known are quite clean, almost obsessively so. 'Glaring,' however, is perfect. Have you ever seen multiple cats— wild or domestic—come together for the first time? Exactly. Cats have glaring down to the finest performance art.

Felis sylvestris catus, or just Felis catus, the housecat, is widely believed to have descended from the Near Eastern or North African wildcat, Felis sylvestris lybica. Though other subspecies of the original cat ancestor are biologically similar and may interbreed, such as the European wildcat Felis sylvestris sylvestris, it was the Near Eastern wildcat who chose to hang around Homo sapiens sapiens as we transitioned from hunter-gatherer nomads to farmers in the late Neolithic period. They suffered our presence for the larder of cat food we created in our new lifestyle, all the varmints who aimed to share our shelter and feast on our food stores—a never-ending supply of rodents, snakes, and birds. These diminutive wildcats crept close to our dwellings, stalked around our granaries, even sneaked into our homes. When we learned of their intentions and their targets, we let them.

Around 3000 BCE, when early farmers moved northward into Europe in search of new lands—not nomads passing through but settlers intending to root down—cats followed. And again, we let them. Even, eventually, invited and then lured them into our homes, hoping they'd stay. They did, when it suited them. The domestic cat subspecies has been traced back to this time, around 3600 BCE. Around the same time, one might argue, as the domestic human. We were trying something new, together. Some took to it more easily than others. A domesticated animal isn't necessarily tame.

I've always been a cat person, from the time at age four when I got to choose my first kitten, a green-eyed, grey and black-striped tabby I named Smokey who let me carry him around like a ragdoll. Smokey and my sister's orange tabby Sixey moved with us after the divorce, and were soon joined by others in those first few single–mother years when we lived in a cottage on a farm and were all in need of furry purring comfort. First a calico named Sugar, then two other nondescript scrappy strays who occasionally came in through the open garage door and up the basement stairs to the bowls of cat food. We let them.

Maybe I first loved them because they were cute and cuddly, like animated stuffed toys. But I grew to respect them for their individuality, their haughty independence, their wild prowess. They hung around when they felt like it, and roamed where they felt like it. To look out to the adjacent field and see a tail twitching in the tall grass and then disappearing, or to watch eye slits widen into black moon pupils as one of our cats paused in the open doorway before leaping into the night, was to have a direct link to the wild. Even in suburbia.

When I was nine and the man who was to become my stepfather moved in and was allergic to cats, we had to rehome all of them. Thankfully, Smokey went to live with my father so I'd get to see him when I visited every other weekend or once a month. But my main home was decidedly lacking in the meowing pitter patter of little feet. So, we begged for a dog—he wasn't allergic to dogs—and after a few uneventful guinea pig years we finally got a puppy. The rest of my childhood years—early adolescence through high school—we were a dog family.

Dogs were okay. Kind of like another sibling—fun sometimes, annoying other times, generally more loud and more needy than suited me, and more my parents' thing than mine. And definitely not… wild.

Canis lupus familiaris, or just Canis familiaris, the domestic dog, is descended from wolves, back in the Mesolithic period when we were still hunter/gatherer/nomads, somewhere between

30,000 to 10,000 years BCE, depending on your source. They sought us out, slunk around our fires looking for scraps, utilized their own social structures to understand ours, even deferentially catching and holding our gaze as they would with their own kind to establish connection and express submission.

Long before dog or human were domesticated, before we'd tamed our food plants and animals, some wolves were tamed. Whether one argues that they tamed themselves or the other way around, the relationship evolved as we did. Wolves became dogs, became guards, hunters, farm help, man's best friend.

In my adult life, I have had friendly, sociable, affectionate cats. Those who seemed to genuinely enjoy my company, to want to be near me, to snuggle by my side and purr when I pet them. But always—always—they retained an air of superiority, making it clear their affection was a choice. They could, and sometimes did, quite suddenly change their minds—lashing out or simply wandering off to chase rainbows, nap in the sun, or roam outside. When my beloved cats would look at me and smile with their eyes crinkling to slits, I felt honored, like a dog getting a treat for being a good girl or a child receiving approval from a stern teacher, knowing I could just as easily, just as mysteriously get the tail-twitching perked-eared wide-eyed glare and brush-off the next second. Though like all of us each cat is an individual, as a whole it really does seem, as all the stereotypes and cartoons and memes attest, like they are humoring us. Allowing our attentions, if it suits them.

Cats just don't appear to need us like dogs do, but instead are using us to their benefit. They won't come when you call or roll over and play dead. If you are lucky they may expose their soft bellies, but you best be ready, at any moment, for teeth or claws.

If our housecats were bigger, they would probably kill and eat us. That was the simplified and popularized takeaway from a series of recent studies that tracked how many victims indoor/outdoor cats do regularly kill, even well-fed cats who don't eat their prey and seem to just hunt for sport. *Not my Fluffy,* we said, until kitty cams proved that even Fluffy was an accomplished serial killer leaving bodies in her wake and cleaning up afterward.

The other relevant studies involved tracking the predominant personality traits of our domesticated felines and finding them consistently aligned with those of undomesticated wild cats in captivity like cheetahs and lions: dominance, neuroticism, and impulsiveness. Have you seen a zoo lion pacing the perimeter her cage, wearing tracks in the dirt? That's neuroticism. Most cats have large home ranges where they roam far and often, mark and protect their territories from interlopers (dominance), and refine their stealth hunting skills (impulsiveness). Our housecats, when we let them, do the same. Maybe they've coevolved with us long enough not to actually want to kill us. But when a clawed arm reaches out from under the bed to swipe at a bare foot, I do wonder: what if the size differential was reversed?

As a birder and naturalist, of course I understand how cats disrupt local ecosystems, that in the woodland landscapes I inhabit, their body counts are more likely to be the ground-feeding songbirds, all fledgling birds (most of whom end up on the ground at some point), chipmunks, and Douglas squirrels, than the mouse pests invading my home. In my adult life when I've had cats, I aimed to keep them inside to protect the wild. But each time, every cat made it clear—they were wild too.

I could see it in their eyes, flashing green or gold as they tracked the action outside the window. I could feel their anxiety as they paced the rooms and stalked me and glared as I stood in the open door. Each time, with each cat, eventually, I relented. And though I felt guilty, fearful for my woodland friends, and may have lied or changed the subject if it ever came up around my birder friends, each time I let my cat outside, I felt palpable, physical relief. As if I myself had just been released from my own cage. Even after the killing started, or when I didn't witness it so pretended it wasn't going on, and even when I inevitably lost those cats to coyotes or bobcats or maybe they just didn't come home one day and I would never know why, I never regretted my choice to free them.

I have heard that there are some cats that do seem to be fine inside. I hear there are those people as well. I am not one of those people, so I guess I don't choose those sorts of cats.

Ancient Egyptians did not worship cats because they were useful animals. Useful animals may be respected, may be shown gratitude, but they aren't worshiped. Useful animals are, most of the time, just used. These days, cats' usefulness in pest reduction is questionable, variable at best. Though most domestic cats seem to enjoy stalking and even playing with their prey, they certainly aren't all effective mousers. They've no need to be; we feed them. Some just play with their mice and leave it at that. Others will create a pest problem where there was none, by going out to catch, then coming inside to release mice, voles, and shrews. Certain small dogs like terriers have been shown to be far better mousers than housecats. We bred them for that. They're trainable. Dogs are loyal, useful animals.

If I'm honest, dogs may have been worshiped too. Or some sort of jackal, anyway, guarding the underworld. But in typical cat-person haughtiness, I'm going to ignore the guard dog deity and focus instead on the wise goddess, the sort of deity I can imagine worshiping. According to the EU's Ancient History Encyclopedia: "The goddess Bastet, commonly depicted as a cat or as a woman with a cat's head, was among the most popular deities of the Egyptian pantheon. She was the keeper of hearth and home, protector of women's secrets, guardian against evil spirits and disease, and the goddess of cats." [6] This doesn't sound like a fully wild animal, not the wildcat, but the relatively new hybrid—the house cat, keeper of our relatively new dominion of hearth and home.

Historians have found that in early Greece and Rome, weasels were kept for mouse control, being far more ferocious and single-minded hunters than cats or dogs, and able to weasel into smaller spaces, as it were. And yet, those cultures also appeared to have welcomed and kept cats as pets. Again, from the A.H.E.: "The Romans regarded the cat as a symbol of independence and not as a creature of utility. Cats were kept as pets by both Greeks and Romans and were regarded highly."

I'm a textbook cat lady: stodgy spinster. Crotchety crone. Frumpy androgynous hag. Eccentric loner homebody. Feminist leftist lesbian–leaning heathen. Mousy bookworm. A glaring of cats lazing around my cabin in the woods would almost be superfluous.

Mightn't a dog fit too, or, instead? Some wolfy husky or willowy greyhound? I just can't see it, any more than I can imagine a husband or kids at my heels. I don't want to be needed like that, and I don't want to need, either. The older I get, the more unapologetically independent I feel. Less like a wife, mother, or dog. More like a cat.

Once upon a time, strong, independent elder women were revered. Especially those in communion with the wild, living earth. Then, patriarchal monotheism turned those earth women into heretics. Anything wild became suspect; anything independent or not fully domesticated—sinful. Bow down obediently to the alpha male, bear his children, live to serve

Him, or suffer the consequences. Feral women became witches; their cats—demons. And then, women became cats—kitten, catty, cougar, pussy.

Independent hunters, never fully tamed. Moonlight stalkers, eyes glowing in the dark. Slit-eyed lurkers, yowling in the alleys. Razor-clawed tail-twitchers, dreaming in the sunshine.

I very much wanted cats. But I just couldn't imagine confining such wild beings to the cage of my house. I have too much respect for them. More than respect—empathy. Yet, I also couldn't imagine releasing such wild beings into the sanctuary of this landscape. I have too much respect—empathy too—for the other wildlings who make their lives and homes out there, and who have also become my familiars—birds, squirrels, snakes, and salamanders. Independence is not indifference. One may resist needing others and still feel empathy, not apathy.

So. No cats for me. Right?

Right?

Well… my resolve was weakening. Despite all my research and reasoning, all the trying to talk myself out of it—all the reasons I shouldn't, I can't—I found myself, increasingly, considering tossing out *shouldn't* and *can't* and going with *want*. On those days when my solitude edged toward loneliness, when my exasperation and overwhelm with the outer world sought some comfort greater than the sight of wild animals or the touch of trees and earth, greater than soft lighting, hot tea, and warm blankets; the thought and memory of furry familiars welcoming my arrival, weaving between my feet or curled up purring on my lap, became an ache with an intensity of *need*.

Maybe this time, I'd find a cat without wanderlust, content to watch from inside. Maybe I'd get two cats who would enliven and enrich each other's lives. Maybe I'd build an elaborate catio where they could breathe fresh air and feel the sun on their fur, safely behind a screen. Maybe these were all rationalizations and excuses and no matter how I did it, the fact remained that I'd be selfishly using other animals for my own comfort. And maybe, though I may never make peace with my selfishness, I might just do it anyway.

IO

Steward

Glove up. Yank out, ball up, and toss a blight of English ivy metastasizing along the forest edge. Pluck the sprouts and excise the root balls of Himalayan and evergreen blackberry infecting the open understory. Amputate wayward English laurel sprouts, saplings and trees, by hand, shovel, or saw. Tweeze strands of reed canary grass from the creek bench.

Pan out, think big, go long. What would happen if you left this land alone, and what might be worth interrupting, removing, or encouraging? Not just for you, but for the overall health of native flora, and for all the mammals, amphibians, birds, reptiles, fish, insects and other invertebrates who live here, or who might one day. How best to tend this landscape?

Salmonberry—quintessential Northwest shrub, magenta star-flowers and first juicy berries of spring, hair-thin thorns protecting even the smallest twigs—surprised you by acting greedy here, knowing no moderation, attempting to take over. New shoots popping up in the few patches of open sunny meadow have got to go. Dense sprouts attempting to inhabit the entire quarter-acre creek bench have to be thinned. Canes shading out the wild blueberries, poking up through sword ferns, erasing your path to the creek, and with the audacity to grow in the gravel driveway will be removed.

When you walk the land with pruners and hand saw, you see differently. You discover dead twigs on red huckleberry shrubs and feel visceral satisfaction in snipping them free. Step back and see the shrub anew, unburdened. Or, you notice how the dense foliage of vine maple trees have begun to block the sunlight from reaching the understory shrubs, the ground covers, and the front porch beyond, and in removing just the right branches you all feel lighter, looser, brighter. Even, you believe, the vine maples.

The ancient overgrown apple trees needed more than simple pruning—after years of neglect and bear climbs they required a complete makeover. During your first winter here, you were too timid, too hesitant, and took too little. That summer the trees sprawled heavy with apples on crowded and weakening branches. Several large limbs cracked.

Your second winter you knew what you needed to do. You spent a whole day with ladder and saw, making large, careful cuts. Stepping back, circling and looking from multiple perspectives. Then snipping smaller twigs, minding the fruiting bodies, noting the angles new growth would take. Trying to think like a fruit tree. And, like a bear.

You had thought that owning land would be like mothering. You were wrong. You are not the older, nurturing matriarch tending a helpless babe. This landscape is so much older than you, and contains multitudes you could spend the rest of your life just beginning to fathom.

You are also not the consummate nurse caretaking a frail grandparent. This landscape is a vibrant, resilient, independent elder whom it is an honor to serve. You're more of a minion, a reverent subject, eager to learn and refine your role in supporting the component parts, as in a body craving nourishment, appreciating cleansing, desiring balance.

Glove up, boot up, wade in. An alder tree, fallen directly across and into the creek, would block salmon passage. Or maybe it wouldn't—they could have jumped it, would have scaled far worse to get this far—but why make them? Why not ease their passing, where you could?

Also, it just felt wrong, that tree, there. The once whooshing, rushing creek turned spitting, splashing, harshly protesting this new wall, exploding over the top. You heard it from inside. Saw the spray. It wouldn't do. Never mind the February cold. Never mind the fierce rain-swollen currents. It had to go. You waded in.

Stepped carefully on slippery rock, stood strong against the thrusting water. Deeper in, against ankles, then shins, then over the boots and to your knees. No turning back. The butt of the tree was wedged against the opposite bank, so you had to go all the way. The alder wasn't thick, maybe six inches at base and narrowing to three, but it was long—formerly tall—probably twenty-five feet. Reaching the trunk you gripped, held, wrestled, and finally freed it, cradled the weight in your arms. You could feel the water struggling against it through the wood. You began to move.

Like a workhorse, you leaned in, head down, and pulled. The current was strong against the tree, against your body, but you were stronger. You walked on numbing legs upstream until the narrowing length of tree behind you finally swung lengthwise into the current, with the flow instead of against it. Only then did you wade the end over to the shallows adjacent to the shore and let it fall. Then moved to the narrow top to tuck that too against the bank.

Back on dry land, shivering, dripping and muddy, you listened, and looked. It sounded right. Looked right. Felt palpably better, like a sliver removed. The downed tree, in its new location, would mean shelter and shade to salmon fingerlings rather than one more obstacle in their parents' way. And, a new perch for the foraging dipper.

Helpful, perhaps, but necessary, for any of them? No. Satisfying? Aesthetically pleasing? Joyous? Absolutely.

Also unnecessary? Planting anything. This is—aside from a few tenacious but sparse invasive species—a healthy Pacific Northwest woodland. After spending years learning and teaching local ecology, then working to restore these landscapes, you could take one look around and recognize that. Recognize individuals. So many old friends from past homes and workplaces—trees, shrubs, and groundcovers, host to butterfly, bird, and beast. And yet, why not use your experience to supplement, beautify, diversify your home? To finally plant something and stick around to watch it grow?

Glove up and dig in. Three red-flowering currant shrubs for the hummingbirds. Three evergreen huckleberry shrubs for the berry enthusiasts, you included. Paper birch and black hawthorn for your Celtic ancestors, and a sugar maple tree for your father. Willow, ninebark, and red-osier dogwood stakes along the far end of the creek bench for diversity, wildlife, and privacy from the neighbors. Lavender, rosemary, heather, and wintergreen off the front and back porches—cheerful companions you've had with you everywhere, but this time, not bound in pots. This time, rooting in the earth. And this was just the beginning.

How to truly immerse in a landscape? Reach back before the idea of human stewardship and remember that whatever else you are and are becoming, you remain an animal among other animals, making your home here. The fact that you are animal with dexterity, foresight, and consideration for other lives doesn't preclude your primal needs and desires, but it does inform your choices.

Glove up and bring scissors, bags, and basket. Snip cedar tips from multiple trees to make a tincture, and collect fallen greenery to make a winter wreath. Pinch off nettle tips just above the joints so that you can enjoy spring's superfood in soups and scrambles but they can keep growing. Pluck new dandelion leaves for salads and sautés, just one or two from each bunch as you move around the yard. Collect just a few berries from any one shrub, leaving plenty for birds, bears, and coyotes.

Walk around the yard with a dish of vanilla ice cream and top it with sun-warmed, slightly tart red huckleberries. Sit against a Doug fir tree and welcome gifts of the land into your body, while all around you, other animals do the same, each in their own ways.

How to love a landscape? Gloves off. Watch, listen, feel, and know what to leave alone. Decide not to buy a mower and let the meadow go feral in summer. Delight in the riot of wildflowers that thrive, the bumblebees and butterflies that frequent them, and the other critters who use them for browse, shade, or shelter: rabbit, salamander, and frog. Some flowers native to this soil, others not, but all finding balance and offering unique gifts.

The colors! From pristine white English daisies to sensual purple foxgloves, fiery orange hawkweeds to dainty powder-blue forget-me-nots. Bold buttercups and dandelions in the sunniest patches, bashful bleeding hearts along the forest edge. Subtle pasture grasses with stunning flowers of their own— greens and purples in an array of shapes and textures, if you look close enough. And you do.

While the neighbors mow and spray, edge and landscape, sterilize and homogenize, you understand that one essential element of tending is simply attending. Knowing when to stop doing and just look, listen, and appreciate. To love the land by noticing, applauding, and delighting in the component parts and the whole.

To actively work the land as a reverent subject. To immerse as an animal among other animals. To notice and appreciate as a contemplative human. These are your gifts, and, your responsibilities. Your stewardship, your ever-deepening relationship. How to make a landscape home.

11

Spawn

Few phenomena are as mesmerizing as a spawning salmon holding steady in a flowing stream. Fire maybe—the liquid undulations of flames in air. But unlike combustion, that chemical conversation between heat and fuel, salmon's communion with water is animate, intimate.

I'd heard some splashing, thrashing noises earlier in the day and finally crept down close to the creek just as the larger male coho—candy apple red with a visibly jutting toothy underbite—moved on upstream. The remaining female held mostly still over a smoothed-over sand and gravel-bed in the otherwise cobbled creek-bottom.

The only way to hold still in a moving body of water is to dance with it. Slow-body wave, slight shimmy, slide, and then a sharp tail-pump to move forward. She turned on her side for a moment, flashing pink, then back upright, nose into the current. If it wasn't for her white tail, she'd have appeared more ripple than fish, a riverine shadow.

Her tail was white because she was dying. She was dying because it was her time—she'd spawned. Buried fertilized eggs in the streambed, her work done. Her body—now more fit for saltwater ocean than freshwater stream—was already disintegrating: battered, pock-marked and scaleless in patches. But she made it, hundreds of miles and through countless barriers. She survived all the toxic chemicals downstream and downriver through town and city to the sea, then back again. She avoided being eaten by all the other fish/birds/mammals/diseases that would love a fish dinner. Journey complete, she needed do nothing more than float, flow, dance her final watch over her offspring until she died. She was coming apart, and yet, she was beautiful. It was an honor to watch.

Days later, I watched my father die. He was dying because cancer was eating his esophagus, his lungs, his stomach, his kidneys, his lymph nodes, and more until his body was disintegrating. In three weeks he'd gone from an active, joyful, astute 79 year-old with no health complaints but heartburn to a shrunken, listless, confused old man, gasping and moaning.

He was supposed to live into his nineties like his father did, we thought, to slowly give out and fade away peacefully, long into the future. He didn't make it.

It all happened so fast that we struggled to keep up with the ever-worsening news from the few doctors he saw, as my sister, who lived nearby, struggled to keep up with the needs of his quickly failing body: from assisted ambulatory to walker to wheelchair to hospital bed almost faster than she could arrange for the equipment.

My father too, seemed briefly optimistic, then dazed, worsening to bewildered, and then, while still lucid, what appeared to be a resigned calm which may have been denial but to me, knowing him, felt more like wise acceptance. Just, holding steady in the stream, because there was nothing else to do but float. In one of the last coherent phone conversations we had, I asked him how he was. He said, "Better than some; worse than others."

By the time I was able to fly out to Montana to be with my sister at his side, he didn't wake up again, had fallen into that restless final sleep/nightmare the hospice nurses called terminal restlessness. Sometimes snoring—as he always had—sometimes choking, wheezing, wailing. His hands, diminished to twisted claws, scratched at his chest, struck out and away, grasping for something or someone we couldn't understand. His breathing succumbed to gurgling, as fluid filled his lungs. As if he longed to return to the watery womb where he began. But, like ocean-acclimatized salmon returning to the freshwater of their natal stream, their bodies have changed too much to live in those conditions again. To return is to die. Always.

He slowed. He calmed. He gurgled, and he stopped.

I'm lucky, people tell me, to have been by his side when he died.

Am I?

I suppose I am glad I was there for him, in case he knew and if that was some sort of comfort to him. *He knew*, people tell me, *and it mattered. It helped.* Perhaps.

But, aside from that unknowable factor, am I glad to have watched him die?

I know this is the part where I'm supposed to find some beauty in witnessing that transition, in watching his dance with death. I haven't. It wasn't beautiful; it was horrific. And now, always, lurking among all the happy memories of my witty, ebullient, feisty father is that shriveled little man already smelling of rot.

The point, I guess, is that my salmon analogy doesn't fit as I wish it would. This isn't about my Zenlike voyeurism in getting to watch an animal's final moments on earth. Not about standing on the creekbank and watching a life peacefully fade away, from the comfort and safety of my separateness. My experience of my father's death was intimate, chaotic, and traumatic.

No matter how close we were, or weren't, through our lives, no matter the changeable psychology of our relationship—that man, my father, made me. My body formed, in part, from his. He allowed my birth, so the least I could do was to witness his death. To listen to him gasp and moan, to hold his clawed and grasping hand. To read aloud, sitting on the rug by his hospital bed, tales of his ancestral homeland. To hold a cold washcloth on his feverish forehead. And, once he'd passed, to dress his shrunken body in a favorite outfit for the cremation.

Those memories hold no beauty, and I don't feel lucky for having them. What I did and do feel is simply the responsibility and helplessness of a daughter, his spawn. Dancing with this visceral, indelible memory of where I came from, whom I came from, and where, one day, I may end up, as I make my own way upstream.

12

Freak

Our excessive emotions are so patently painful and harmful to us as a species that I can hardly believe that they evolved. ... It would seem that emotions are the curse, not death— emotions that appear to have devolved upon a few freaks as a special curse from Malevolence...

– Annie Dillard, from *Pilgrim at Tinker Creek*[7]

I stepped out on the back porch in the raw February morning, inhaled the musty air, eyed the remnants of last night's rain still dripping from the firs, and clutched my heart. That pain, again. The vice on my chest that I can't decide whether to name grief or anxiety, unsure if I'm holding back a cry or a scream.

I was fairly sure I wasn't having a heart attack, or heartburn, or Covid, or some other physical ailment, as my cholesterol levels were low, my heart healthy, my digestion decent, my lungs clear. Psychological, then? Reasons enough in recent times—my father's death, the extended pandemic, the climate crisis, catastrophic fires, the firestorm of white supremacy and misogyny, the latest mass shooting… those were the big ones, the good reasons for all manner of obsessive thoughts and painful emotions.

And yet, I'd lived in this body long enough to know that the origins of my emotions aren't always logical, aren't so neatly named. I had felt this exact pain at times when there were no good reasons at the ready, so I was left casting about for some chemical or hormonal imbalance, the wrong food, the wrong lighting, the weather, ancestral or spectral influence, something on the wind…

So. More pressing than how to name the pain was what to do with it. How to get away from the panicky feeling bubbling up and threatening to spill over, and over, and over, unstoppable.

I would have liked to physically get away, could have used a road trip, camping trip, extended backcountry expedition (Pacific Crest Trail, perhaps?), a foreign vacation. A journey away from eddying thoughts, my own weary voice. But real escape, even as a relatively unencumbered child-free middle-aged woman, isn't always possible. The day job required my physical presence and I required that job to pay the mortgage. Most cultural activities and social diversions outside of computer screens were still shut down or too overwhelming for an introvert, and local public trails were crowded with so many other stir-crazy humans heading into another year of pandemic variants that those places felt about as safe and soothing as a hospital waiting room during a full moon.

I exhaled a silver cloud. It swirled into the mist rising from around the row of ninety-year-old Douglas firs with needled limbs perched so far above my cabin that I only know their stout ridged trunks, so large I can barely wrap my arms halfway around. Beyond the trunks the moss-covered earth slopes down and away toward the creek—in flowerless winter, a soft Kelly-green expanse punctuated by grey lichened twigs and darker green fir branchlets, storm-severed and blown down from above.

Chickadees' soft *chick-chick* conversations reached me from a brushy young hemlock, their staging area for trips to the feeders. Otherwise, all I could hear was water. A few drips and drops here and there, but mostly the rushing creek. That swishing, shushing, whispering white noise undercurrent of home, that constant soothing reminder of that other world, out there, down there, nearby.

It helps. I've sought out rivers, creeks, and streams since I was old enough to seek them. Whether they were a walk, a drive, or a hike away, I've found them. My favorites are the churning whitewater rivers or cobbled brooks, complex and textured, not those slow wide sloughs with little to say. I regularly and repeatedly visited those near enough to my homes. The Nubanuset River in New Hampshire; Boulder Creek in Colorado; Sandy, Clackamas, and Breitenbush rivers in Oregon; Skagit, Skykomish and Stillaguamish in Washington. Spending time with any of those old friends always helped.

All right then. It is our emotions that are amiss. We are freaks, the world is fine, and let us all go have lobotomies to restore us to a natural state. ...Perhaps I don't need a lobotomy, but I could use some calming down, and the creek is just the place for it. I must go down to the creek again. It is where I belong...[8]

I must go down to the creek again. Though I could hear and see a glimmer of the creek from my back porch, it wasn't enough. I needed to get away. To leave *here* and go *there*, journey to another world, the Otherworld that might pacify me, ground me, restore me.

So, I went.

I pulled my wool hat down over my ears and zipped up my jacket, but took off my socks, left them on the porch. Then, stepped down onto the cool moss, bare feet touching earth, soft earth touching me.

I walked carefully on winter-tender soles across the sodden green sponge of sloping yard. Slowed when I reached the shrubby flood plain path to the creek bench, eyes on the leaf litter in an attempt to keep to the slick mud and not blunder onto sharp remnants of cut salmonberry root or prickly trailing blackberry vine. Finally, I reached the smooth round stones of the creek edge, the hard cold of rock laced with the grit of sand.

Two minutes, tops, even at the pace of naked feet, but I had entered a different world. Swollen with rain and early spring snowmelt, my little creek was at its most riverine—racing, tumbling, flinging itself over boulders and around logs, eager to greet the larger river less than a half-mile downstream. From my vantage at the water's edge, I could look right and see upstream maybe only thirty yards where a curve brought it out of deeply cut banks in the dense forest, ancient conifers growing out of even more ancient eroding stumps. Looking left I could see about the same distance downstream where the water flowed around another corner through twiggy salmonberry and lanky alders at the edge of the neighbors' properties. Directly across the creek in front of me rose pole-thin cedars, hemlocks, and a thorny thicket that buffered me from those neighbors and completed the effect of standing in my own private forested amphitheater—the water the stage, the main act, the big show. I was a spectator, a fly on the wall, a speck of stardust.

In summer or in full rain gear I might settle down onto the river stones, but in the raw wet of February I retreated to the iron chair I'd tucked back against an old cedar stump on the edge of the creek bench, chair legs dug into sand and anchored with rocks so it won't wash away in high water. I picked off a piece of wet moss, did my best to swipe off any pooling moisture, and sat.

At my feet, a ribbon of river stones gleamed silt gray, but the longer I looked the more colors I saw—jade green, salmon red, speckles and stripes of black, white, and indigo. That small strip of stones would be completely submersed in higher water, an extension of the river bottom, while in summer it would become a wide rocky beach when the stream shrunk to its most diminutive.

Stream, creek, brook, river... I vacillate over what to call this kinetic flow, knowing that the naming is in the eye—and cultural context—of the beholder. I've consciously chosen not to use the name on the maps, a colonialist surname that says something about a long-dead European and nothing about this living landscape. I haven't been able to find the Indigenous name, so I mostly just call it the creek. Sometimes, *my* creek, though I realize I am but a brief visitor, I too a colonialist droplet in the span of this waterway.

What I'm getting at is movement, direction, and, on a human timeline, permanency; the faucet is always on. That a landscape can continually, constantly, collect and channel enough water to create a reliable, consistent—if changeable—flow is nothing short of extraordinary.

Glacier-fed rivers make sense to me, maybe because I've witnessed their origins. Hiked up mountains to where waterfalls gushed from just below massive ice sheets near their peaks, starting the journey downslope, collecting ground and rainwater on the way. My little creek's thin blue line first appears on the maps just east of me in the foothills, little more than a mile from where I see it emerging from the upstream bend, the entire meander of it far below glaciers and permanent snowfields.

Does it bubble up from underground? Seep out of the moss? Where did all this water come from, really? What if it stops?

I rested my eyes on my favorite riffle, a satin pillow of water that seems to be present no matter the season, sensual curves like a former lover's neck, low back, and hips, a reminder of my younger days when I could think of little else. That lover is long gone, my desires waning. That riffle will change. The river will move, and eventually, one day, will stop.

I sighed, and closed my eyes.

I retreat—not inside myself but outside myself... I am the skin of the water the wind plays over; I am petal, feather, stone.[9]

All I could hear was water. Not a single unified instrument but the whole orchestra. Or perhaps, a jazz band. From my chair at the front of the amphitheater, rumbling rushed in from my right and retreated to my left like a drumroll. Closer and more subtle were guitar *bloop bloops* from rocky riffles straight ahead and bass-like gurgling somewhere off to the left. Those were the loudest, the most insistent, but the longer I listened the more I heard the subtler sounds, simmering cymbals of distant rapids and piano plinking of tiny ripples lapping over pebbles near my feet. All that music received simultaneously, not just with my ears but my whole body—felt sound—like the reverberation of the best summer concerts.

Except it was winter, and instead of cheering I was pretty sure I was working up to some sort of breakdown.

But then, a new sound. Liquid but not of the water. Melodic but not of an earthen instrument—not just a sound, but a voice. Ringing out, singing out, not in competition with the creek sounds but in perfect accompaniment, a sharp tumbling forth of whistles, trills, warbles and burbles, starting and restarting, choppy and churning, like the rocky creek herself. I opened my eyes.

There, perched on a mossy rock jutting barely above the flow in the middle of the river slightly upstream, gangly toes gripping the sprayed surface and slate-gray body bouncing in time with his song as if the power of his voice shook the very earth beneath him, stood *Cinclus mexicanus*, an American dipper. *My* American dipper.

I'd heard him before—his liquid metallic chiming rising up from the creek sporadically throughout the year, always catching my breath in my throat. Just to know he was here, this "water ouzel," voice of cool, clean rivers of the American West, this songbird who swims, just to see the gray flash of him winging upstream, following the contours of the water just above the surface and then suddenly plunging down deep always leaves me agape in ways that other birds rarely do.

But why? Plenty of other birds—waterfowl and more typical shorebirds—know intimacy with water, land, and air. But watching ducks in a pond or sandpipers on a mudflat doesn't stir my breath, heart, or sense of awe like a dipper on a river. The dippers I've known are at home in my favorite landscapes: Sitka spruce-shaded streams of the Pacific coast, old growth-remnant whitewater rivers in the Cascadian foothills, or crystalline-icicled mountain streams of Colorado, Oregon, Washington.

Maybe it has something to do with the patent vulnerability, the freakish audacity of that solitary little songbird who dares to dance with a raging river, not content to exist on earth, in the air, or on the water, but to know all three at their most tumultuous. To see from multiple perspectives, to dip and dive and go deep, to know the darkest depths and still, to rise up singing. And to do all this, usually, alone, even in the depths of winter, even before any hint of spring.

Maybe, I envy him. Maybe, I want to be him.

I stood. And slowly, so as not to spook him, I stepped toward the creek. Bare feet on cool stones, and then, into the icy stream. The cold was shocking but not painful, not immediately. Enough to make me suck in air between clenched teeth and blow it out through pursed lips.

What struck me more than the temperature was the power of the water. Even just up to my shins I could feel it pushing me, threatening to take me down, so I splayed my legs and strengthened my stance, heels dug in to the sand between stones.

The dipper gave a few shrill shrieks and moved to a rock slightly farther upstream, bouncing and peeping. I ached for him to stay with me, wanted to seem unobtrusive as possible, so I looked away, down at the water curling around my cold-reddened legs, my toes clenching sand.

Then, on a whim, I started bouncing. Deep knee bends as the dippers do.

The current thinking about this quirk, this tic, is that the dipping helps them see underwater, to change the refraction of light in looking from different angles, the better to spot their next aquatic insect meal. Other scientists suggest it also serves as body language, a territorial pronouncement to other dippers who might be in the area. My hunch is that in addition to the various biological reasons for this, like any adaptive behavior—like singing, or sex—perhaps, also, it might just feel good.

Once I started bouncing, I found it hard to stop. It kept me warm, for one, but it was also, somehow, calming. That vice on my chest started to loosen, a little.

Dipper began to sing again. Three clear whistles followed by a short trill, a metallic rattle, two down-slurred tones, another rattle like a tin bell, and more whistles, more trills, and on, and on, all effervescing from a feathered grey being the size of my heart.

He sang, and we bounced.

And then, I started to cry. But almost simultaneously, bubbling up from deep in my own body, came laughter. I laughed and cried together, a sharp tumbling forth of liquid warbles and burbles, stopping and starting, choppy and churning like the creek itself.

This is what I had come for, just this, and nothing more. A fling of leafy motion on the cliffs, the assault of real things, living and still, with shapes and powers under the sky—this is my city, my culture, and all the world I need.[10]

This is why I'd come. My journey, my pilgrimage to the creek was just this: re-immersion in the world of real things. To see from new perspectives, to dip and dive and go deep. And to do all this, not alone, but in concert with others. With the complex voices of a rocky creek, with a bold and hearty aquatic songbird, with another solitary seeker's words written almost forty years ago and over three thousand miles away, and with all the other kindred spirits carrying their burdens to their own wild waters. We freaks, we pilgrims at our creeks, shall plumb our darkest depths and rise up singing.

13

Wayfinder

I sliced off a thorny tangle of salmonberry shrub and tossed it aside. Yanked up a young elderberry and tore off a ragged handful of sword ferns. Exchanging pruners for the handsaw in the back pocket of my Carhartts, I sawed away a vine maple limb. Heaved a rotting cottonwood log as far as I could manage, and punted a tangle of fallen hemlock branches.

Sometimes, I feel like the Tasmanian devil in that Warner Brothers cartoon—the spinning top of a beast that whips into a frenzy and speeds off to destroy everything in his midst, an animal tornado. I move somewhat slower and am continually apologizing to plant and fern, tree and displaced bird, but the frenzy is there, urging me on. I like to believe I'm creating something new, something worthwhile, but another part of me fears I'm just another modern human: encroaching, violating, desecrating.

I started forging trails when the pandemic began, and as the mutating virus persisted, I just kept at it. It got me out of the house and moving in nature, and felt safer than braving crowded public trails with varying assemblages of masked and unmasked, vaccinated and unvaccinated, bottlenecking together at every switchback.

It is a relatively gentle trail-building as these things go. No heavy machinery involved—just pruners and a handsaw—and I aim for the easiest way through in an attempt to avoid the larger, longer established flora. But this is no open eastern woodland; this is a dense, tangled quagmire of second-growth Pacific Northwest understory, approaching my idea of a jungle with vines, thorns, and saplings all around, such that I could often use a scythe. Then I could really whack away at it all, reaping... what? Space, I suppose. And distance. And possibility. A way through the chaos, away from what was and toward what could be.

Trail metaphors are the most well-worn of clichés. Which doesn't make them any less valid.

I am trespassing—let's get that out of the way too. The woods immediately adjacent to my property belong to a neighbor down the street. Beyond their expansive plot lies state land, then Forest Service land, all the way into the North Cascades mountains. I feel okay about the trespassing part. I'm not doing any major damage, nor making any permanent changes that wouldn't erase themselves after a year or two of negligence. I don't think anyone would mind? Not that I'm going to ask permission.

Steller's jays' grating complaints erupted from down the trail across the skunk cabbage wetland barely visible through dense foliage. I paused my destruction to attend to them. A wren *chip chipped* closer to me.

Aside from wren and jays, the September afternoon was quiet. I sat on a fallen alder trunk, cocked my head to listen better, and squinted toward the jay ruckus. All I could see was a wall of green—sword fern, salmonberry, vine maple, red alder, and devil's club—and all I could hear were the insistent wren and squawking jays.

Was I the disturbance, or were they reacting to some other animal I'd awakened, disturbed, displaced? A weasel, perhaps, or a hawk? What about bear, or bobcat? I looked over my shoulder at the slender ribbon of open forest behind, looked up at the thick branches of maple and cottonwood above, gripped my tools a little tighter, and resumed clearing the obstructions ahead.

I had nearly a mile of trails by that point, data I'd confirmed with a mapping app that plots and saves a GPS course through any terrain with cell service, which, so far, I had. My first trail was a loop that entered the woods near the creek and paralleled it for an eighth of a mile through downed hemlocks, scattered cedars, vine maple tangles, and thorny salmonberry walls. It then curved up a rise through a congregation of devil's club and angled back toward my property through upland cottonwoods, bigleaf maples, and the edge of a cascara and nettle-lined wetland.

My second project cut a spur off of the uphill edge of the first loop, weaving through Oregon grape and sword fern understory, skirting the edge of the wetland to a well-graded strip that would become my third project—an old logging railroad path built up between two swampy wetlands, confirmed by a small extrusion of rail jutting out like exposed bone at a long washed-out stream cut. To my delight, this linear path led me west to a neighbor's cleared four-wheeler trail where the work had been done for me. Their trail ran south again to a more recently cleared and traversed logging road, from which I circled back a ways and then forged a new and easy trail down beneath dense silver firs, cedars and hemlocks back to the railroad grade, completing a second, larger loop.

I'd thought I was done, but then, something about that railroad graded berm nudged at me. I'd only followed it one direction— west toward neighbors. Could I just let that eastern stretch toward the mountains remain a mystery, not knowing where it might lead? I could not.

A blowdown of branchy cedar, hemlock, and a collateral cascara blocked my path. I sawed at a limb then lobbed it away. Then another, breathing in the resinous sapwood as it met the dappled sunlight. I continued until all that was left was a large section of a cedar trunk on the ground, and I stepped over it. I rubbed sticky fingers on dirty pants, pulled a twig from my hair and re-cinched my matted ponytail. I would be brushing moss out of my hair again that evening.

I've been thinking about the recently named though ancient practice of Forest Bathing. Though a part of me can't help but smirk at the commodification and monetization of simply being in a forest, I do get it. I have felt it, emotionally and physiologically. I have read some of the multiplying studies on the various mental and physical health benefits of walking or sitting meditatively in a forest. How the color green soothes anxiety. How just fifteen minutes of quiet forest time lowers breathing and heart rate, blood pressure, and cortisol levels. How trees give off phytochemicals for their own communication that also work on our brain and body chemistry, including physically boosting our immunity. How the complex textures of the living world give our racing data-dulled minds a rich alternative that simultaneously relaxes and rejuvenates, our animal bodies reveling in the living world we spent tens of thousands of years evolving in and from which we've relatively recently extricated ourselves.

I have chosen to live in a forest with an increasingly conscious understanding of all of the above. It works. It helps. And, sometimes, it isn't enough just to be, here. Sometimes, I couldn't sit still if I wanted to. I need to do more than just bathe in it. Increasingly often, it seems, I need to dig in, tear out, cut up, Tasmanian devil myself into that forest, that forest into me.

More than the other trails I'd made, my rail-trail seemed already in use by others. Not by other hominids—not for decades—but by other mammals. As overgrown as it's become in the intervening years after abandonment by the logging company, it remains a flattened way, elevated above swampy depressions and without larger trees or stumps. Still the easiest way through for bipeds and quadrupeds.

Though graded wide enough for a train, I sought only to clear the width of a human. I found, on that old railway, my width was often clear already, as if some other, shorter, Tasmanian devil had preceded me. In those places, I needed only follow those who'd come before, and expand the height. Or occasionally, when the taller obstructions were too large for a handsaw or too rare and vibrant for me to feel okay with cutting and there seemed no other way through, I left them. As a result, a traverse on my rail trail is more of an obstacle course of climbing, shimmying, limboing, and even, here and there, morphing into quadruped and crawling through.

A deer track here, a raccoon handprint there, depressions in a downed log as if used as a stepping off place for generations. A bear-scratched cascara here, a bear-gnawed fir there.

Even off the old rail way, I was beginning to realize I hadn't been forging new paths as much as discovering the paths already there. The easiest way through had already been found and regularly used by more agile, more spry bodies than mine. All along, I'd just been enlarging them. Clearing them of obstacles. Just like old times, in my jobs as park ranger and natural areas technician. Except this time, using my opposable thumbs and metal tools in service of those who have none. Which isn't to say they needed my service. But that first winter snow when I discovered coyote tracks traversing the entire lowland loop, intermingling with those of raccoon, deer, and a single mysterious bobcat track, I felt like maybe these trails might be enjoyed by more than just me. Not necessary, but utilized. Even, appreciated.

Jays erupted again ahead of me, from the as-yet uncleared for humans end of the rail trail. Angry and persistent, concentrated at a single point in the veiled woodland. Closer this time. This time, the hair stood up on the back of my neck.

I froze, and stared into the quadruped-cleared tunnel in the thicket. Looked up above me, all around, and then down. I squinted at the earth in front of me. And suddenly, like a magic-eye poster morphing from a jumbled pattern into the clear outline of recognizable object, I saw something.

Just ahead—I had almost bumbled through it—were two parallel scrapes in the leafy duff, piled to one end, creating a rectangular tableau that just a few years ago would have meant nothing to me, but thanks to a wildlife tracking class, was now clear as a billboard announcement, a blinking neon sign. The visual and olfactory territorial announcement of a large-eyed, blunt-nosed stalker.

I knelt down and smelled the pile, thought I caught a whiff of something, which for my weak human sense, meant this was a fairly recent calling card. A large cat scrape. This scrape, too large for bobcat. So? Cougar.

Good grief; I was on a mountain lion trail. Cougar was *here*. Cougar *is* here??

I decided to heed the jays' warnings and my own intuition to leave off clearing for the day, and backtracked to my connector trail down past the wetland toward the lowland loop home.

I walked slowly, all senses alert. I stopped every few steps to look back, up, and around; I sniffed the air; I listened to every snapped twig, bird call, or rustle in the leaves, and to the messages coming from my own body.

Emerging from the forest into my yard, I felt like a different animal than when I'd left. I walked up my driveway and collapsed against the cedar by my front steps, exhausted and elated. Muscles comfortably sore, and typically racing mind—quiet. I felt more grounded—meaning, specifically, physically and energetically more wholly in my body—than after a quiet walk or meditative sit in the most serene landscape. All along, maybe what I'd really been clearing was the way back to myself.

I placed my buzzing hands on the earth and felt the support of the tree at my back. Then, I leaned my head back and stared up into the feathered sprays of cedar boughs, finally content to be still. Just to be.

14

Supplicant

Candles flickered softly in the pre-dawn darkness, casting a warm, golden glow across the room. My radio, a 1980s-era AM/FM receiver that had belonged to my father, broadcast "Sunday Sunrise," the local classical station's reverent choral music show. The coffeemaker clicked, hummed, and sighed away cheerfully; the aroma of coffee beans with a hint of the cinnamon and cloves I'd sprinkled on the grounds mingled with the honey-sweetness of the beeswax candles. In baggy pajamas and holey LL Bean slippers, I walked over to a bookshelf and knelt.

It was a special day. The day before, I'd finished a book, so it was time to choose a new one. The thrill, the anticipation!

Once upon a time, before printing presses allowed mass production of the printed word, books were relegated to the elite. The one percent, we might say today. Private libraries of bound volumes were a sign of prestige, the fine china or sportscars of yesteryear. And though buying books remains a privilege not available to everyone, it is possible nowadays to amass a physical library as a humble citizen, a cabin dweller in thrift store clothing.

Thriftiness and limited space restrict my purchases to books I know I'll read soon. I always keep a ready supply of at least a few unread books, just in case. Books, like the stocked cans of soup on my kitchen shelves, feel increasingly like necessities. Food, water, shelter, and books. Not trifles to borrow and return, and certainly not digital files to read on yet another screen, like work—the horror! Physical, bound books are investments, treasures, soul food. To have, and to hold.

Which isn't to say that I keep every book I buy. I have regularly purged my book collection, bringing some to Powell's used book counter to sell, leaving them in Little Free Libraries or thrift stores, or giving them to friends if I don't think I'll read them again, if the books don't bring me deep joy, insight, or solace of some kind. The books that stay are thoughtfully chosen and curated.

The fiction shelf is small because I read less fiction and often give those books away afterward. I might have enjoyed the story, but not have felt the deeper resonance to make me want to hold it close. A few favorites that have made the cut include Brian Doyle's *Mink River*, Willa Cather's *The Song of the Lark*, Ursula LeGuin's *Buffalo Gals and Other Animal Presences*, and Marion Zimmer Bradley's *The Mists of Avalon*. They have become like friends.

My poetry collection is also small and shifting; the sparseness and brevity of that genre just don't offer enough density for me to sink my teeth into. As powerful and moving as poetry may be in the moment, it is more likely to float through me and continue on, and so do the books that contain it. A few that have remained include Mary Oliver's *New and Selected Poems*, Robert Sund's *Poems from Ish River Country*, and William Stafford's *The Way It Is*. The poetry shelf shares a bookcase with fiction, and both sections have ample empty space.

Nonfiction spans four cramped bookshelves. One holds a reference section of dictionaries, thesauruses, writing craft tomes, runes & other ancient scripts, Celtic history & folklore, and health & healing. Another is packed tightly with field guides and natural history books on flora, fauna, and ecosystems of the various landscapes where I've lived and explored. A third hosts psychology, ecopsychology, and spirituality. And the final, perhaps most beloved stacks amass personal essays, memoirs, and personal nature writing. A veritable congregation of contemplative, navel-gazing truth seekers.

I agree with the idea that there is always a degree of truth to be found even in the most fantastic fiction. However, nonfiction, by definition, carries a deeper level of honesty—seeking and revealing meanings found in lived experience. And this, for me, is the main gift in reading. Not to escape real life, but to experience it through others' eyes. A book as a world of wisdom and insight from another striving human working through their whys, hows, whos, and wherefores. And as such, my nonfiction books are more than friends; they are teachers, guides, gurus, soulmates.

Books, of course, are just one way of exploring human experience. And yet, for me, a book feels like the most intimate way in to such revelations. Even more, somehow, than if the writer was here with me. Content on screens, on stages, and even from the mouths of live humans remains out there, over there, separate, and all broadcast with so many other sensory, contextual, and cultural cues that the words themselves can get bogged down, diffused. Whereas, curling up with a book in my hands, the stories seem to come from within, embodied, as close and clear as my own internal voice, just speaking different words. The author's experiences, their explorations, become as my own, and my life is richer for them.

That day, in choosing my next read, I wanted deep truth. An articulate, wise, yet humble voice of a fellow explorer. A book that would readjust my frame of mind, even shift my very reality, such that when I put the book down and looked around, everything would be different, though I hadn't left the couch. I wanted a pilgrimage of the mind.

And so, kneeling, I chose. I chose a book I hadn't known where to shelve—memoir or psychology or Celtic spirituality— which wouldn't change even after I finished the book. But I would know in the first few pages that it would be a keeper. I would know that once again, as if guided by larger forces, I'd picked up exactly the right book at exactly the right time in my life. The book was *Crossing to Avalon: A Woman's Midlife Quest for the Sacred* by Jean Shinoda Bolen.

The title was almost too perfect, too obviously right for me, though I knew that didn't necessarily translate to all that I'd find inside. But oh, it did. I highlighted and underlined, added notes and exclamation points in the margins. In reframing a woman's midlife transition not as a crisis but a quest akin to a grail quest, I wondered, then imagined, then knew that I was in the midst of my own renewed search for meaning, depth, and coming of age on the path toward elderhood. As Woman. As aspiring crone.

Bolen's Jungian-informed mythologically-framed memoir of her personal pilgrimage wouldn't likely be for everyone. It might not have been for me until recently; I might have found it equal parts too analytical and too woo-woo. She wrote it as part of making sense of her own journey, turning over her unique experiences with her unique intellect and insights. She wrote it seventeen years before I picked it up. And still, it was as if she was writing for me, speaking to me. Asking, *what path are you on, and who are you awakening into on that path? What sacred gifts for the world are you carrying, now? What new call must you answer?*

I would pick up her book from my bedside table in my 4 a.m. perimenopausal insomnia. I would bring her book to read against a cedar tree on a cliff overlooking the Salish Sea. And I would pick up her book from the couch in the evening after workday doldrums of emails, spreadsheets, and Zoom meetings. And I would, every time, be changed. Not by her world and her words alone, but by the cocreation of our minds together. Our pilgrimage.

Not every book resonates so deeply, but each is a quest in its own way, a holy vessel. And we as readers are called to fill it, with all we are and who we are becoming.

15

Muse

Awake

In the predawn darkness, dreams still swirling in my mind, all the world quiet except, perhaps, for a lone owl calling from the rain-soaked greenwood, I get up to write.

Breathe

In, and out. Calm and clear the monkey mind that seeks, always, to take over—to plan, prescribe, and proclaim. Make room for a different voice, a practice more mystery than plan, more precarious than solid, but always, in the end, the right one.

Coffee and Candles

Ceramic mug on the slate coaster, that first hot sip always the best. If the writing is good, the coffee will go cold before the cup is half empty. One soft yellow lamp and a collection of earthy votives and beeswax tealights. Swirling, spiraling steam. Flickering twinkling flames. An invitation, an invocation. A call.

Dipper

Words arrive sporadically, like dippers at the creek—suddenly, stubbornly present, vibrantly chiming, flighty and changeable as the creek itself. I best pay attention, engage while I can, before they vanish back into the opaque flow, leaving only ripples.

Examined Life

Not a conscious decision so much as a compulsion. Even an addiction. Meaning as a knotted muscle to pummel and knead. A scab to pick, and pick again though it bleeds. Shelves full of spiralbound journals. Three memoirs and counting.

Fifth grade

Mr. Coghill assigned my first autobiography. Invited my first self-reflecting, crafted telling, and reworking until it felt right, until it felt like me. Until I had something to step back from, look at, point to. The deep satisfaction of physically holding and owning my own story.

Gratitude

"...pay attention, then patch
a few words together and don't try
to make them elaborate, this isn't
a contest but the doorway
into thanks, and a silence in which
another voice may speak." –Mary Oliver[11]

High School

Ms. Lacoss conducted my first creative writing class. Helped me to feel the words, immerse myself in them in ways I hadn't before. To seek delicious, visceral adjectives, verbs, and nouns, and join them in surprising ways. To delight in my own writing, as if it came through me, from elsewhere. Perhaps, a muse.

I

I wonder. I seek. I ask. I listen. I receive. I reflect. I remember. I celebrate. I grieve. I rage. I accept. I understand.

I write.

Journal

The playground, the workshop, the therapy room. Occasionally documenting details, but more often processing reactions, emotions, insights, and my very sense of self.

Kingfisher

Perches above the creek, rattling, chattering, ruminating, musing, and muttering. Eventually, she dives under, goes deep, and if she's lucky, seizes treasure. Most times though, she comes up sputtering, shakes it off, and resumes rattling, chattering, ruminating, musing, and muttering.

Liminal

In the flow. In the zone. An altered space. Altar space. Zen.

Looking up from my writing, I find the world changed. Brighter, clearer, new. I am simultaneously more connected with and less affected by everything.

Muse

Greek goddesses of literature, science, music, and the arts. Water nymphs worshiped at sacred springs. Mountain peak demigods, whispering in our ears. Inspirational guides, external sources of wisdom and creativity.

Neuroscience

"All this points to the probability that the earliest marks were aesthetic in that they derive from the early visual cortex's preference for basic configurations. And it could have begun as early as *Homo erectus*, which lived from about 1.8m to 500,000 years ago."[12]

Oregon

Resting against a sun-warmed rock at the top of Tom McCall Point in the Columbia Gorge, journal open in my lap, gazing out across a field of butter-yellow arrowleaf balsamroot smeared with lipstick-red Indian paintbrush, through wind-stunted oaks and over rocky cliffs to the azure river below, having just scrawled three pages of reflections on place and people and myself among them, I decided/realized/accepted, maybe for the first time—*I'm a writer.*

Processing

Musing, ruminating, contemplating, analyzing, working through, working out. Introspection not just about me, but about all of you, all of us, all of it. All the time. A primary characteristic of sensory processing sensitivity, or the "highly sensitive person" (HSP) trait. Also common in generalized anxiety disorder. And borderline personality disorder. And the twenty-first century. And writers.

Questions:

Who am I? What world is this?
Who are you? Who are we together?
Who am I now?
And now?

Read

Wildlife tracking was the first form of literacy, animal signs our first books. Scent marking, feeding sign, claw marks or antler rubs on vegetation, scrapes in the soil, and tracks in the mud. We learned to read, first, in order to eat and not be eaten.

Story

"There is a story in every thing, and every being, and every moment, were we alert to catch it, were we ready with our tender nets; indeed there are a hundred, a thousand stories, uncountable stories, could they only be lured out and appreciated; and more and more now I realize that what I thought was a skill only for authors and pastors and doctors and dream-diviners is the greatest of all human skills, the one that allows us into the heart and soul and deepest layers of our companions on the brief sunlit road between great dark wildernesses." –Brian Doyle[13]

Time

Like a photograph, writing can freeze time. Unlike a photograph, writing can also move backward, and forward, and back again. Writing can travel to times where we've never been, and may never be.

Urania

The Greek muse of astronomy, but also data analysis, universal truths, philosophy, and dreamers. Feet on the ground and head in the clouds, always seeking the big picture, the panned-out view, the science and the mystery behind it all.

Voice

Though the writing seems to come through me, this voice is always recognizable as my own. A truer, clearer, elder self, speaking from the deep quiet of another realm, uncluttered by the noise of the everyday.

Wilderness

We are all explorers of wondrous, treacherous, untamed and untamable landscapes. Some of the most expansive may only be found in the intangible realms of our minds, where we might catch glimpses when the lighting is just right, when the right words appear.

XYZ

Letters, alphabets, writing—just lines in the sand, scratchings on paper, shapes on a screen. Simple tools for the mysterious, miraculous rites of reaching out—or in—to the universe, finding meaning, and making it last. Writing is magic.

16

Anchorite

In autumn I succumb—edge up the heat and close all the windows. As the final window clicks tight, I feel a brief twinge of panic. I've shut out the birds' twittering chatter at the feeders, the drips and plops of rain on falling leaves, and the gurgling creek not yet swollen with winter showers. I've shut myself in.

Inside, all is quiet. The quiet, is loud. My ears are ringing with it, like electrical wires humming in my head.

I've noticed loud silence before, but never the ringing, never aside from immediately following the few loud concerts I'd attended in my younger days. Most of the time I listen to music quietly. My hearing is acute, seems to be getting more so as I age. I can listen to hushed voices in private meetings through closed doors. I can hear the subtlest, highest-pitched bird sounds from far in the distance, and my own heart beating inside me. "Owl-ears," I've been called. But this ringing— it's new.

It could be menopause; tinnitus may be associated with hormonal shifts. Maybe two traumatic brain injuries and tmj disfunction are catching up with me; ringing ears are a common result of head and neck trauma. Stress exacerbates tinnitus. Ear-ringing has also been found to be an emotional response of a body seeking to tune out fear, especially from past emotional trauma or an unsafe environment. Each a plausible physiological explanation for this static in my head, none particularly useful in what to do with it.

It could drive me batty, this ringing.

It would be easy to drown it out, leave the radio on during waking hours. Eclectic, independent, alternative rock on KEXP; soothing classical on KING; or old timey bluesy jazz on KNKX, all curated by real live DJs—music and voices to fill the void. I do, sometimes. Until that, too, feels too loud. Seeking quiet, I turn it off, hear the ringing. Turn it on again— too loud. I've become the cat who wants to go out, no—in, no—out, no…as if there's some in-between place she's trying to reach, that is neither.

If you put your ear to a tree in early spring, I've learned, you might hear the sap running, rising up from the ground close to the surface of the bark. Last year I tried this with a hemlock in my yard, and was able to tune in to the hum of the tree's insides, to hear a sort of rushing sound, like an underground river. Now, nearing winter, as trees pull their energies inward, downward, underground, even real owl ears couldn't hear their stories. You'd have to be inside a tree to hear them.

I am inside the hollow of my own tree now—cedar planks enclosing me in warmth and dryness—and I am grateful for that. And though I do miss the natural noises I now have to leave the cabin to find, the longer I sit inside with the resounding quiet the less I choose to block it out. The more I am drawn to it, as if summoned. Even, compelled.

Maybe it's time to go deep, to tune in to the silence and follow where it might lead. I don't mean just this time of year, but this time of my life. What whisperings might I hear in my own depths; what stories might emerge from my own inner river?

The refrigerator's cooling fan clicks off. A baseboard heater's metallic tapping pauses. A faucet releases a single drip into a glass bowl in the sink. I take a deep breath, hold, let it go. Embrace the silence. The ringing is louder.

I look around the room at all the comforts here, the safety in objects, the objects another sort of noise. A thrift store couch, my father's desk, a hand-me-down bookcase, an Ikea table. An assortment of chairs, blankets, pillows, rugs. Wall hangings, houseplants, candles, journals, books. Colors, textures, depth.

I close my eyes, let them go. Embrace the darkness. The ringing is louder.

Inside, I find—a cave.
I know this place.

Abandoned silver mine
turned bat hibernaculum
turned graduate research project.

From crystalline snowy morning
to sultry mineral night.
Crouch, crawl, then stand,
eyes adjusting
to the underworld.

Elfin mammals
glistening with condensation
adorn the walls
like diamonds.

Hearts slowed.
Breath sporadic.
Nearer to death than sleep,
no epic months-long dreams
churn in those bright minds.

They've gone elsewhere
in search of different dreams,
profounder visions.

I follow.

Find the in-between place
of bats, cats, and ancestors—
ancient Buddhist, Viking, Mayan…
earlier Mithraic, Paleolithic cave questers

Not the vision quests of heroes
on lofty mountain peaks
but hermits, eremites, anchorites, troglodytes
self-entombed in the hollowlands,
etching stories on the walls.

I follow.
Behind the resonant echoing drips,
beyond the thick, moist breaths.
deeper into the cavernous blackness.
An opening, a portal.
Crouch, crawl, then stand.

The quiet—expansive
the ringing— louder still.
I know this place.

Descent unto death?
Hell?

Choose your own adventure,
your mythology
religion
gnosis.

Hel, pagan goddess of the underworld,
subterranean otherworld.
The dark interior realm not of suffering,
but transformation.
Even, rebirth.

No sky god there
but earth mother,
Great Mother,
Crone.

No cup—a cauldron.
No tomb—a womb.

From this vessel—
dissolution
gestation
transformation
regeneration.

Reverberations
in the hollows within
and without,
the resonant hum of the universe.

It's all there,
ringing out.

I am inside
listening
biding
becoming.

I open my eyes, welcome the light. The colors, the comforts, the warmth. The ringing remains.

Stress? Head Trauma? Menopause?

In some cultures, some circles, ear ringing is a sign that the soul or psyche is tuning in to higher vibrations, accessing new spiritual realms. A sign of good fortune, spiritual awakening, third eye opening, contact from angels or spirit guides.

I don't know if I believe all of that, or any of it. Yet. But the older I get, the more I'd like to. The more I'm willing to listen to all the possibilities, flowing within.

I am listening still.

17

Heathen

What are you, classmates asked me in grade school. As a white kid surrounded by a majority of other white-appearing kids, I knew they meant the other primary categorical difference we learned young to attend to: *what religion*. While the suburban New England towns where I grew up weren't the bastions of religious diversity of the metropolitan areas nearby, you still couldn't assume, and in the progressive public schools I attended, we recognized and learned about multiple religions and religious holidays.

What are we, I asked my mother. We didn't attend services of any kind, but we did celebrate Christmas and Easter, if you count the decorated tree with gift exchanges in winter, and colored eggs, chocolate, and stuffed bunnies in spring.

We aren't anything, she said, once she understood the question. I pressed her, insisted, believing religion was like ancestry, a biological fact passed down through generations. Which it seemed to be, in some families, some cultures. Just not ours.

Finally, perhaps to shut me up, she told me she was raised Protestant. Which did shut me up for a time, until I realized that answer didn't mean much aside from a non-Catholic Christian, encompassing so many different belief systems as to be another form of non-answer, and not really describing anything we discussed or did (or were supposed to have done) in our home. The kids who asked the question and cared about the answer knew to ask the follow-up, *what kind of Protestant?* I never did find out, or if I did, I forgot soon after, because I was beginning to understand that belonging to one of those particular clubs came with certain knowledge and beliefs I just didn't have. I eventually decided that *I'm not anything* was probably the better answer.

So, you're an atheist?

Yes, I'd say. *I'm an atheist.* If I didn't belong to any of the religion clubs, I must be an atheist, right? I so very much did want to belong, somewhere.

Turns out, I wasn't a very good atheist either.

In ninth grade I asked for a small gold cross to wear around my neck. I knew what that cross meant and that I didn't believe any of the dogma behind it any more than I believed in Santa Claus or the Easter Bunny. Mostly it was a continued effort to fit in, to adopt some of the customs of the ruling class (i.e., the popular kids) in order to feel less like the nerdy misfit band geek I was becoming.

And yet. That cross around my neck? It felt different than any other necklace I'd worn. It felt… powerful? Resonant? Magic? Even, sacred.

For a year or so, until my drama club/skater boyfriend gifted me a blue stone pendant from the new-age store I'd begun to frequent. The stone, a six-sided obelisk, was made of the mineral sodalite. On the little card with it were the words *For Intuition, Balance, and Clarity*. I believed it. I felt it. Power. Resonance. Magic. Sacred.

Until a year or so later, when my Italian mafia-idolizing boyfriend lent me his gold St. Christopher medal pendant. For protection. I believed it! I felt it!

Just, necklaces. Mere trinkets. And yet something in me sought, and found, something deeper in each of them. Something bigger than me, my boyfriends, my species, my reality.

Feeling/sensing the sacred in everyday objects is as old as religion itself. Carved figures, statues, symbols, sanctified buildings, shrines, sacred roads. Whether and how many others believe as you do determines how you will be judged: pious, apocryphal, sinful, even delusional.

I did go to church a handful of times, with my mysteriously Protestant maternal grandparents, and with a Catholic friend or two when I happened to be staying over on a weekend. I felt like the alien I was; I tried my best to follow the strange customs, mouth the words to the songs and chants at the right times, to sit/stand/kneel and smile and shake hands when appropriate and generally wished myself invisible as with most large-group social situations. As for the sacred, I felt nothing. Those churches—just buildings. Those pontificating men— just men, telling stories.

We read part of the old testament in my seventh-grade public school English class, as a "work of literature." It was the first time some of the formal beliefs based on that book started to sink in; I began to analyze it because I was asked to, and as a foreigner to those beliefs, they both sounded absurd and not even the sort of mythology I'd ever want to believe in. Why did so many people believe? Why did so many *women* believe? The Greek myths we read next sounded equally plausible and felt less personally oppressive somehow, despite the recurring violence there too. Why not them? Because of who won which wars thousands of years ago?

I wouldn't have said any of that then; I could barely articulate it to myself. Even then I knew it was dangerous territory, that I would risk alienating a powerful majority of my fellow humans (power, not numbers, being the key factor.)

And now? I guess I'm ready to say it. When encountering any of the major, monotheistic religions of the world, whether in their places of worship or expressed beliefs, it isn't just that I don't feel any sense of the sacred, it's that I feel an overwhelming sense of authoritarianism. Or to be more concise, patriarchal tyranny. The in-group, the popular kids, the ruling class, the elite, venerating a royal father figure who hoards resources for obedient insiders, and judges, denounces, punishes and destroys outsiders. Major religions as politics, same-same. Their God or Lord or savior or holy man, just another changeable, unpredictable, abusive father figure. In Dad they trust. And I just… don't. Father issues, obviously.

Which, of course, is the judgment of an outsider. I've got it all wrong, they will say. Their true beliefs, their true religion, isn't like that at all. And I understand that, at least, that there is something I am missing there, something they feel that I likely never will.

So. Definitely not a Christian, or Jew, or Muslim. Therefore, by some definitions, I might actually be deemed an atheist. And yet, I would counter, I'm assuredly not.

In my teen years, that time of seeking belonging and deeper meaning, what I'd felt in those necklaces had more to do with something waking up in myself. That adolescent learning to look both inward and outward and beginning to understand that there was more to this life than the mundane. That the path and roles laid out for a woman, for a human, by religions, by culture, by socialized modern society were all just stories, and that there were deeper mysteries at work in being a human animal on this earth. Maybe if I could explore them, I could find my own path, my own roles to play. Or not to play but rather, to live, genuinely.

That sense of the sacred, each twinge of mystery and depth, served as an invitation, a choice. A potential path. Some of which, when explored, led to dead ends. That gold cross and that St. Christopher medal I quickly realized were someone else's paths, never mine. They quickly went cold, felt false. So, I kept exploring.

In college I took a course on eastern religions, dabbled in Buddhism and Taoism. I hung Tibetan prayer flags, perched buddha statues on my bookshelves and drew yin yangs in my notebooks. Those didn't last long either.

I joined the Pagan Student Union and enjoyed the rebellious smugness of pissing off the conservative Christians, who were many at the University of Virginia. Pentagrams joined the yin yangs in my notebooks. I don't remember anything we did in the group, mostly potlucks I think, and among the self-named Wiccans and Druids I felt almost as much a fraud and alien as I had in church. No overt patriarchal dogma this time, but a more subtle in-group entailing specific rituals, a generally antagonistic attitude, the right clothing and jewelry. In my jeans, t-shirts, and hiking boots, eager to please and getting good grades, I didn't feel subversive or defiant enough for that group. More, the rituals discussed felt like the childhood seances and Halloween dress-up I felt I'd outgrown; I felt no real sense of the sacred there.

There is still something in the tiny silver pentagram earrings I'd purchased then. I take them out and wear them now and then, feel a little charge. That five-pointed star enclosed in a circle having nothing to do with the devil—a primarily monotheistic idea I don't even believe in—but the Goddess. A mysterious earth-mother energy that has always held some resonance, if vague and tentative. But eventually I feel like a fraud wearing them, not knowing enough of the stories behind that symbol to have earned them, and worried about what others might assume or expect of me, so I put them away again.

That blue obelisk necklace also remains in my jewelry box and comes out more often from among other earthly talismans: amber, silver, agates, and moonstones. Unlike the cultural symbols laid out by others before me, I feel free to infuse them with my own meanings. And I have, I do.

What am I? My mother was right. I'm not anything. I follow no customs, observe no religious holidays, worship no one or nothing. But I do believe in something bigger, have faith in Mystery, and even, for lack of a better word, Spirit in all things. That force that infuses me with life, that makes me more than a machine of separate parts, more than neurons firing in my grey matter. And not just in humans or other plant and animal lives, but in all aspects of our earth: rocks, rivers, and entire landscapes. A certain thusness that makes each one an individual, numinous being. Not because I read it in a book or was told by an authority figure, but because of my felt sense of experiencing the world, in my body and some deeper knowing beyond that.

These days, mostly, I feel it at liminal times, in liminal spaces. Moments that slow time, invite me in, make me feel both small and part of a greater whole. That twinge of mystery, beauty, evanescence, ensorcellment.

I feel it in the luminous mist rising into sunlight after an early autumn rain. In the high C of the frog song chorus in spring twilight. That one sensual riffle in the creek that always draws my eyes. The impossibly intricate, delicate pink curl of a foxglove blossom. The flash of the crown of cottonwood trees still in sunlight at 9 p.m. on a summer night, while the world below lies in dusk's shadows. Spending an afternoon on my belly watching a slug consume a mushroom, slowing the very earth on its axis. That cedar tree in the forest with a mossy smiling face grown into the bark. The chickadee who dropped to my level, cocked his head and eyed me with one beady little eye. The moment after waking from a dream, knowing I'd travelled far that night. A mossy sylvan glade in the Pacific Northwest. A redrock desert in the arid Southwest. A wolf tree in a clearing in a deciduous woodland in the Northeast. An echoing swamp in the sultry Southeast. A cave. A mountain. A river. The sea.

Silence. Presence.

Power. Resonance. Magic. Sacred.

Sunday morning pre-dawn sits with coffee steaming and candles burning, preparing to write. To write, as I do, a way of making sense, of working through ideas and experience. But also, I'm realizing, a way to get closer to this vague Mystery, to the Sacred. To try to name the un-nameable, to hold the unholdable. Paying attention, reverence, humility and awe as forms of worship. Probably, the earliest forms. The older I get, the less I need to categorize it, or fit my sense of it into that of others around me. To glimpse it, to feel it, even in the briefest moments, is enough.

18

Lunatic

Who am I? I am not and will never be anybody's mother. I have often been transient. I am Goldilocks living in a fairytale cabin among her bears. I am a loner grandmothered by a tree. I am witness to my wild neighbors who witness me back. I am a queer spinster, an antisocial hermit, and a menopausal hag. I have always been a cat lady, with or without any cats. I am the steward of a landscape, spawn of the earth, swimming upstream to die. I am an emotional freak. A spastic trail-building wayfinder. A supplicant to books and the muses of contemplative writing. I seek meaning within as an anchorite and beyond as a heathen. I am becoming a crone, and I plan to survive that.

All of this I am, and more. And yet? As I move through perimenopause and solidly into middle-age, my sense of self feels as fleeting as the mist rising from my roof when the rain gives way to sunlight. I've tried on identities like so many pairs of shoes, in and out of relationships and landscapes and schools and careers and still, even three memoirs in, struggle at times to see myself clearly.

Turns out, unstable sense of self and struggles with identity are one of the nine diagnostic criteria for borderline personality disorder. The feeling of being a chameleon, a fraud, of always feeling like an outsider, or as BPD scientist Dr. Marsha Linehan puts it, "the I don't fit in disorder." Of course, that quality alone doesn't signify mental illness. For some adults and most adolescents, unstable sense of self may be uncomfortable and challenging but not necessarily symptomatic of anything other than self-awareness. The need to ask *who am I* and *where do I belong* on a regular, even daily basis just seems to stick with some of us more than others, because any answers we discover turn out to be ephemeral. So, we keep asking.

And yet, for my 49th birthday, I was gifted this very label—borderline personality disorder—and found, to my surprise and even relief, that it fit. Not just like a pair of shoes, but deeper, more elementary, like finally relocating my feet. Like looking in a mirror and seeing a core part of me clearly for the first time.

I'd sought out a therapist for support after my father died suddenly and other smoldering relationships flared into firestorms, all at the time of early pandemic lockdown, apocalyptic climate crises, racial unrest, rising mass shootings, and other cultural stressors that could give any sensitive human panic attacks. But after ten months of weekly therapy sessions that quickly went beyond immediate stressors back to my childhood, down extensive rabbit holes of developmental trauma, sensory processing sensitivities, dissociative stress responses, chronic impulsivity, unstable relationship patterns, trust issues, anger issues, and general mood instability, it became clear there was more going on with me than recent hormonal shifts, something that might be worth delving into if I was game. I was. And this time, rather than me grasping at something and trying to make it fit me, my therapist eventually, cautiously, and gently offered up this new label, and asked what I thought.

My first thought? *Finally. It's about time.*

Some part of me had always known, though the counselor I saw for cutting at age sixteen didn't name it. *You're just sensitive.* When I read the description in my Psych 101 textbook three years later and clearly recognized myself, I was told, as well-meaning professors tell all new psychology students, *you're not one of them.* Over the years when I hinted at my struggles to others who never saw the full picture of me—because I never showed them—I was dismissed, repeatedly. My well-meaning therapist mother? *You're not one of them. You're just sensitive.*

I am sensitive. Thirty years after that first psychology class, I finally learned what else I am. Many people who believe they know me will be surprised. A few key friends, teachers, most ex-bosses, and the few romantic ex-es I was with long enough to later be considered ex-es, will not. *Finally. It's about time.*

I had to do my research, of course, and my therapist helped me find the right sources, the recent and thankfully now relatively extensive and promising resources, studies, and personal stories.

Though it remains one of the most stigmatized diagnoses, with much misinformation out there and even dissent among professionals about whether it is a valid diagnosis or should be reassigned to the bipolar spectrum, a variant of PTSD, or suck-it-up-and-get-over-it-you're-just-hypersensitive, I've chosen to focus on the parts that resonate and the sources that validate. When you've asked yourself your whole life *what is wrong with me* and are finally offered an answer backed up not just by psychology but biology, accompanied by promising treatment options beyond medication, you pay attention.

I easily met seven of the nine DSM-5 criteria at the time, and could see that at the most tumultuous points in my life I had experienced all nine, while in my calmer times I would have been down to three or four, below the magic five required for diagnosis and officially just hypersensitive and moody with borderline traits. But rather than go into all those clinical minutiae, here is what fits like magical glass slippers on newly visible feet: BPD is a long-term pattern of emotional, interpersonal, behavioral, and occasionally cognitive dysregulation. It's chronic hyper-reactivity to interpersonal or environmental stimuli with the inability to effectively self-regulate or self-soothe, stemming from a combination of genetics (including family history of BPD), other biological predispositions, and, usually but not always, developmental trauma involving primary attachment figures.

From the brain science realm, it's an overactive amygdala—the primal emotional reactions center—combined with an underactive prefrontal cortex—the logical reasoning center, in conjunction with an exaggerated cortisol response that kicks you into fight, flight, freeze, or collapse at the slightest provocation. It's being told your whole life—not just when tired or hungry or stressed like everybody else— that you're overreacting, that it isn't that big a deal, let it go, stop being so sensitive, stop being so rigid, why are you so angry, calm the fuck down… which you would very much like to if only you knew how to tame your inner beast who is somehow you and not you. It is lashing out at others as if possessed, and the leaden guilt and shame when you come to in the aftermath. It is bracing against cataclysmic internal storms just long enough to function appropriately in public, then imploding catastrophically when finally alone, turning all that caged lion-sized rage against yourself like you believe you deserve. It is feeling like a raw nerve, an emotional burn victim, an emotional hemophiliac, walking around with your heart outside your body despite how it continues to get battered with all your frantic efforts to love and be loved until, fearing the next heart stomping could kill you or someone else, you withdraw into whatever sanctuary you can find, and hide out there where at least it's safe.

I am borderline. This new identity doesn't describe all of me any more than any of the other labels I've tried on over the years. And yet, the parts that fit, seem, somehow, to describe much of what I've been exploring for three books and counting, and even why I write in the first place. I write myself into being, again and again. I have to.

Does adding this label suddenly, magically end my quest for who I am and where I belong? It does not. Is it a piece of the puzzle? It is. And not one of those random lucky middle pieces, but part of the framework. Even, a corner.

Other than naming it as I've done here, I'm not sure I need to write much more about my particular torments and gifts of BPD because I can see now that all this time I've been doing exactly that. Not just chronicles of dysfunction and dysregulation, but narratives of coping, healing, and regulation, foremost of which involve my deep relationship with the natural world, perhaps my primary and only secure long-term relationship.

Why name it at all then? Considering the ongoing stigma proliferated by media and antiquated clinicians alike that we are all vindictive, manipulative, empathy-deficient lost causes, and considering the risk of being pigeonholed as my diagnosis, all other identities and complexities of me lost in the shadow of Mental Illness, it's a risky choice. And maybe, that's exactly why I need to do it. For all the sensitives, hyper-reactives, traumatized, and sensitized regardless of diagnosis, who might resonate with some of what I've shared. But most of all, for others like me, hiding in plain sight. You matter, and you are not alone. [14]

19

Crone

The chill in the morning air felt like autumn, smelled like autumn, though it was barely mid-September and the dry day was expected to warm into the 70s. I pulled my blanket around me and leaned back against the cedar, eyes trained on the apple trees. No sign of the bears yet, but based on the apples' ripeness, I expected them any day. In another couple months when the rains had settled in and the creek was high again, I'd be looking for salmon, listening to the dipper rejoice in the exuberant flow. Chickadees would have replaced the purple finches and black-headed grosbeaks as the primary feeder visitors, and the Douglas squirrels would be feverishly collecting dropped seeds and tossed peanuts to stash away for the winter.

It felt good to know my place well enough to anticipate what was to come. Though I realize nothing is certain, that change comes regularly—faster now—and that everything seems increasingly precarious, that just makes what remains, what returns, that much sweeter.

That day, I was in the in-between time. The waiting time, both ending and beginning time. Liminal space. I strained my ears to hear the soft trickle of the summer-quiet creek. I breathed in sun-dried cedar and dew-damp earth. I dug bare toes in dry dirt and tilted my head back to look up at the branches above. I felt both rooted and restless. Both at home and in exile, in community and yet apart from it. I was getting used to that feeling.

I hadn't bled in almost a year. I had no children, no partner. I lived alone on the outskirts, the witch at the edge of the village. Once upon a time, I might have been shunned, banished, even burned, for not fulfilling my duties as a woman, for not bowing down to a man. Once upon a time, I might have been locked up, drugged up, and forgotten for my rages, my compulsions, my sensitivities, my defiance.

Once upon a different time, I might have been welcomed into a place of service, of wisdom. I might have become merchant, healer, midwife, historian, priestess, peacemaker, poet, or counselor. In these times, in this place, I am forging my own path, making my own choices. Or at least I aim to try.

From behind me, a meow. A question—*meow?*—intended, I know, for me. I stood, stretched, folded my blanket, and walked back around the cedar to my porch, where a newly built catio enclosed two, year-old feral rescues who'd just come out through their cat door to their fenced half of the deck to greet the morning. Freyja, a rotund black beauty with golden eyes, and Loki, a rambunctious grey tabby with green eyes, noted my presence and went back to taking in the air, monitoring the birds and squirrels, and awaiting the first shafts of sunlight they would later bask in like royalty. I left them to it and went back inside.

I pulled on a sweatshirt against the lingering cold, put on the kettle for tea, and realized my hot flashes had been fewer and farther between. My rashes, less frequent. My physical body seemed to be calming. My moods, however, were as erratic as ever. Emotional storms, stronger. Unapologetically ranting, raving, crying, laughing, eating, emoting. Maybe a part of me was still in transition, or maybe this is who I really was, who I am, finally the crazy cat lady I was always becoming. As unsettling as that might be, whether or not I ever finally settle into a stable sense of who I am, or at least a calmer version, I do know that I feel more fully alive than ever before, and increasingly at peace with uncertainty. For now, I remain on my midlife quest, the spinster at the end of the lane in her woodland cabin on the creek, retreating within, sitting outside, wandering, witnessing, stewarding, reading, writing, and listening my way to the answers—grasping at meaning, as I always have. Maybe, in time, that is where wisdom lies.

20

Survivor

I am a frayed and nibbled survivor in a fallen world, and I am getting along. I am aging and eaten and have done my share of eating too. I am not washed and beautiful, in control of a shining world in which everything fits, but instead am wandering awed about on a splintered wreck I've come to care for, whose gnawed trees breathe a delicate air, whose bloodied and scarred creatures are my dearest companions, and whose beauty beats and shines not in its imperfections but overwhelmingly in spite of them, under the wind-rent clouds, upstream and down.

–Annie Dillard[15]

I was worried about the cedar. The elder western redcedar standing guard by my front steps—my cedar. The red-breasted sapsucker had tapped a dozen or more new dotted lines into her skin and she was bleeding. Standing at her feet, looking up, I saw linear punctures and glistening amber sap drips everywhere, as high as I could see and down close to my face. I could hear him, hidden high in the canopy, making more. *Tap tap tap.* Pressing both palms flat against cinnamon bark, I could feel it—the subtle, steady violence. *Tap tap tap.* I did want the sapsucker to thrive, and recognized that one way or another, all lives consume other lives. But this was too much.

How much can one tree handle? How many wounds, how many scars?

Pencil-thin white line up my left forearm from wrist to elbow: punched through a glass door at age five.

Slightly rosier, droopier flesh of my right cheek: crashed my bicycle with full impact on my face; scraped off cheek on pavement at age twelve.

Branching latticework on my left cheek, left upper lip, and right chin: mauled by the family dog; jaws sunk deep into my face shredding skin, muscle, and nerves at age twenty-two.

Quilted white pleats beneath my nose and scarlet depression at the bridge of my nose: blacked out and slammed face into pavement, again, after fraught family funeral and too much wine at age thirty-seven.

Bold ruby chevron, seven inches long, bisected by twenty-nine white stitch lines on my left forearm: fell from a ladder and caught arm in taut wire, slicing it open like a raw steak at age forty-seven.

Tiny threadlike lines, barely visible, on my inner ankles, left hip, inner left wrist, and above my left breast: self-inflicted cuts, over multiple years. Not to die, but to make living bearable.

The outer bark of a tree is a rigid protective layer, an armor to shield from wounds and harmful invaders, and to maintain internal water balance. It can be anywhere from a few centimeters to several inches thick depending on the age, species, and survival strategy of a tree. Though the common thinking is that the outer bark is "dead," as long as it remains on the tree it maintains interaction with tissues underneath. As thick as it might be, it remains permeable at certain points, with tiny holes for air exchange.

Under the armor are circulatory systems that transport sugars down from the crown and water up from the roots. The cambium growth layer processes sugar and water to create new cells to replenish the circulatory system, the inner heartwood—skeleton—and the outer bark—armor.

Despite that armor, sapsuckers tap into the thicker, stickier surface sap running strong in late spring and summer—in this region they seem to love cottonwoods, willows, and redcedars—both for nutrients in the sap and the insects attracted to the sap. A variety of other animals, such as hummingbirds, also make use of that ready source of extra sugar and protein. Humans tap into the thinner, waterier sap running strong in late winter to cook down into sweet syrups; maples are standard, but birches and other trees may be used.

Damage to a tree's skin never heals like new. Technically, it doesn't heal at all, though may get covered over with new bark, hardened pitch in some conifers, or most often, edged with thick, discolored scars as a tree attempts to seal off the vulnerable living tissues within. Ecologists and trackers use tree scars to decipher animal sign, environmental wounds, disease, and other damage, to understand some of a tree's unique story in their unique ecosystem.

Human skin is a soft protective layer, to shield from chemical and bacterial invaders and maintain internal water balance. It can be anywhere from a few centimeters to several inches thick depending on a person's age and the location on their body. As thick as it might be, skin remains permeable at certain points, with tiny holes for air exchange. Though the common thinking is that the outer, protective flattened skin cells are "dead," as long as they remain on the body they maintain interaction with tissues underneath.

The outer epidermis contains varying amounts of melanin, for UV protection, and nerve cells, for sensation. DNA repair enzymes help heal UV and other chemical damage, a sort of physiological armor. Under the epidermis are the dermis layers, including circulatory systems to bring sugars to and remove wastes from organs around the body. More nerve cells and hair follicles further assist with sensation. Collagen and elastin provide support and elasticity in conjunction with cushioning protection of fat layers below.

Approximately one thousand different species of bacteria make their homes on our skin's surface, a whole microbiome scientists are still working to understand. When in balance, they seem to live in harmony with a human body. When the surface of the skin is ruptured, however, whether scraped, punctured, or gouged, that balance is lost; vulnerable inner tissues are exposed to invaders from the outside surface or the air beyond.

In healthy skin, blood brings healing fluids to clean a wound, then clots into scabs to seal it from open air. Strong white fibers of collagen then form the basis for new tissue to grow from the inside out, slowly filling the cracks and joining with surrounding healthy skin. In larger wounds where new skin can't bridge the gap successfully, that ropey collagen remains as scar tissue. Scar tissue may seem tough, like armor, but its diminished capacity as integrated skin makes it less strong, less physiologically protective, and less resilient than the original skin.

In addition to the fluids circulating under a tree's skin, the starchy, nutritious cambium layer is also utilized as an occasional or staple food by those herbivores and omnivores who can access it: voles, squirrels, rabbits, porcupines, beavers, deer, ancestral and feral humans, and bears. I once gnawed on cambium from a newly fallen, shattered cottonwood tree. It tasted like honeyed celery.

Without armor, a tree would be eaten alive in no time. Not just by the megafauna, but a whole cadre of invertebrate, bacterial, and fungal invaders eager to feed on the body of a tree.

I stumbled on an ancestral bear trail. I felt foolish for not recognizing it immediately; I had just chosen the easiest way through the forest from the overgrown logging road down a mossy slope to the old railroad grade just above my property. In part, the deep shade of western redcedar and western hemlock in that section had impeded the typically dense salmonberry thickets common in more open understory. But more than that, the earth seemed worn in the way of regular use, my every footfall finding dimpled impressions in sloping ground as solid as stairs. Unlike the active bushwhacking I'd done involving copious climbing, ducking, weaving and tripping through the forest, through this section I merely walked, slaloming wide arcs among conifers, barely needing to lift my feet or move a branch. And then I noticed the trees.

At the base of at least half of the hemlocks along my route were large scars, the sort of broad yawning gouges you might find along a forest road or suburban trail where heavy machinery regularly hacks back the encroaching flora and nicks the trees. In this case, however, the heavy machinery was a bear, or bears, and the hacking wasn't trail maintenance, exactly, but cambium feeding.

Some of the scarred trees had died and stood naked—leafless skeletons. Many of the trees were still alive. While the feeding areas were large, often approaching half the circumference, few of them spanned completely around the tree. To cut around the full diameter of a tree is to "girdle" it—to sever all circulation such that a tree will certainly die. Losing a large section, a deep gouge of bark and living tissues down to the dead heartwood will stress the tree, leave it open to a whole host of other challenges, but need not kill it outright. The resilience of an individual tree depends in part on the environmental conditions and other external stressors the individual has faced. And, each tree, like any living being, seems to have its own unique and mysterious drive—to live, or to let go.

I squatted down next to one of the damaged trees and ran my hand along the scar. The outer bark had grown thick lips over the living tissues, sealing them off from open air, leaving only the dead heartwood exposed. This tree had feeding sign on both sides, so that only thin swaths of living tissue remained, stripes of potential life. I looked up to determine whether this tree still had green needles, but through the lower dead branches— common even in living conifers—the overstory was too dense from multiple surrounding trees for me to tell whether any of the greenery belonged to my tree. My hand on outer bark and scars, I couldn't tell whether she still lived, whether the wounds had, finally, become too much to bear.

I have skin cancer.

Or, rather, I had it. They cut it out of me. A basal carcinoma above my lip and melanoma on my inner thigh. Despite consistent use of sunscreen, despite living on the rainforest edge of the left coast, my skin had failed to protect me from the cumulative effects of UV radiation. *You're young to have had two skin cancers,* they told me. As I hobbled through the surgical dermatology waiting room after the second excision, the only non-whitehair in the room, I didn't feel so young.

Basal carcinoma is a stupid cancer, I learned, the sort that doesn't tend to spread to other parts of the body. They're common in elders. A surgical dermatologist cuts them out, stitches you up, and keeps watch for new ones, no big deal. Mine was thin so that scar was relatively small, spanning the distance between under my left nostril and where the red of my lip begins.

Melanoma is a big deal, a smart cancer that begins on the skin but will seek to go deeper, travel farther, consume a body from the inside out, if it can. So far, I was lucky. The growth was thick but hadn't yet spread—stage two, in skin cancer lingo. The doctor cut deep and wide to be sure, removed a large chunk of flesh and left a double layer of stitches above my right knee, an angry-looking gash the length of my hand. I was to return for full-body skin checks every three months for the foreseeable future. It is likely there will be more, and if I am to survive them, we will need to find them early.

Subtle red highlight on upper lip between dog bite scar and second faceplant scar: basal carcinoma excision at age forty-eight.

Thick black scabs enmeshed in puckered crimson and white folds on inner thigh: melanoma excision at age forty-eight.

I'd been removing old wire fencing from my property. Not from the edge next to the closest neighbors—I'd like all the boundaries there that I can get. I'd been pulling wire out of the forest edge, an unnecessary and potentially harmful barrier to the wild. Large squares of wire fencing the bears had long since pulled down in areas anyway, to get to the apple trees. And rusted remnants of barbed wire, sporadic and sparse, a danger to any unsuspecting or unaware animal wandering between meadow and forest. Including me.

In thick gloves, armed with pliers, wire cutters, and sturdier bolt cutters, I excised the wire. It didn't come easily, much of it buried in years of forest duff with young shrubs rooted around and growing through it. I pulled, I cut, I pulled some more. I unraveled, cut, and finally removed multiple sections and coils of wire. With each extrication I felt relief, almost visceral, as if thorns removed from my own body. The more I removed, the more the need grew in me to get it all out, to feel it gone. Even the parts buried in the earth that likely posed no harm to any of us. I knew they were there.

Following a strand of barbed wire along the ground, I came to a tree. Not just any tree, but the grand old maple tree, the one branching into seven different trunks, each the size of a full-sized three, so thick with old-growth moss that I can sink an arm in almost up to my elbow before reaching bark. The maple that stands guard at the southeast corner of my property, leafy crown seeming to create its own atmosphere, dripping maple rain long after the sky's precipitation has stopped, long after all other trees have dried.

The barbed wire disappeared into the tree, and reappeared on the other side. That it was too late to remove it is an understatement; the wire appeared to be several inches under the outer bark, nary a scar or blemish, no sign of it except where it went in and where it came out. I snipped the wire flush with the bark on both sides and felt some relief in removing the lines from each end, but I knew it was still in there, inside the maple. I ached to imagine it there, inside. Does the maple? Or, is it long forgotten, as inconsequential as the army of bacteria living on my skin's surface?

My melanoma excision wound wasn't healing as it should. Though it didn't seem infected, the wound remained open, scabby, and angry-looking, two months later. Dissolvable stitches can take anywhere from a few weeks to several months to be fully broken down and absorbed by the body, depending on the materials they are made from, and I wasn't sure where I stood on that continuum. It could have been normal. But normal or not, the fact remained that something foreign remained inside my leg, and my skin seemed stalled in an in-between place, unhealed.

Wounds may have difficulty reaching the scarring phase if unclean, as the body gets stuck in the phase of attempting to purge and remove invaders. My leg, it seemed, recognized the stitches as invaders, but hadn't yet been capable of processing them—breaking them down, obliterating them. Instead, scabs formed, shed, and regrew. Tiny points of plastic-like material poked out, and I snipped them off with nail clippers. A week later, they poked out again in the same spot. One day, I pulled a knotted bundle out of my leg, and it bled, then scabbed, anew. I seemed to be failing at the human skill of healing, but couldn't manage the tree skill of compartmentalization. The middle ground? A festering wound, vulnerable to everything.

My middle-aged body has had a lot of practice in healing physical trauma. More than most bodies might experience in a lifetime. I would think that would make me better at it, skilled. But how much can one body handle? How many wounds, how many scars?

The older a tree, the thicker the bark, and the more resilient the living being, the better able to seal off wounds, to recognize and effectively react to invaders. Experienced trees may, scientists are learning, even change their physiology to further protect themselves, such as making their sap and cambium taste bad. They send chemical messages on the wind and through mycorrhizal root networks to warn neighbors, and they receive messages the same way. They can't run, so they've gotten really good at shielding and fighting. And, when harm befalls them anyway, they compartmentalize—seal it off—as best they can. My cedar tree is probably going to be okay, at least from sapsucker assaults.

The older a human, the thinner the skin, the less resilient the living body, our physiological shield less elastic, increasingly vulnerable to lacerations, punctures, infections, and UV damage. Where is my wisdom? What protections have I gained for the years lived in this soft shell?

Unlike my cedar, my maple, the firs along the bear trail, I am not bound in place. My means of protection, I know, is to gain the wisdom first to distinguish what constitutes actual danger, and then to move out of the way when it comes for me. To take better care of how and where I place my body, to better recognize the potential for harm and take what precautions I can before it's too late. It's exhausting, and sometimes, isn't enough. Ladders fall. Dogs bite. Glass shatters. Cancer spreads. Fury possesses me like a demon and I lash out blindly, still. I often wish I had thicker skin, even, bark.

And yet, this gnawed and scarred body lives on. Rootless and mobile, free to wander with the bears, to reach out and touch and be touched by other bodies, whether wrapped in bark, feathers, scales, or skin like mine. That alone makes this tender, armorless vulnerability worth the trouble.

But. I think I am finally starting to want more than just to survive. Not just to get along or wander about or touch this splintered wreck of a world until I succumb to whatever will take me down. I recognize that some dangers, probably most, are beyond my control to prevent. Some wounds are beyond my capacity to heal. But not all of them.

In this aging body, this thinning, marked skin, a desire is stirring. Even, a need. I want to reach in, grab hold, and yank out the festering stitches. The barbed wire. The cancer. Past trauma. From my own body, from this landscape, and from others like me and different from me. Before it's buried so deep that it's too late.

Here, grab on, and let's pull together.

Ready?

Acknowledgments

I am grateful to the editors of the following publications, in which earlier versions or excerpts of these essays first appeared: "Grandmother" in *The Wayfarer Magazine*, "Hag" in *Herstry*, "Steward" in *Plant-Human Quarterly*, "Spawn" in *Pacifica Literary Review*, "Freak" published as "Pilgrims" in the *Dark Mountain* collection: *ARK*, "Muse" in *Shark Reef Literary Magazine*, and "Survivor" in *The Examined Life Journal*.

I am grateful to all the wise women and feral elders who have come before me—human and more-than-human. Thank you for being my teachers, role models, and guides on this path, leaving breadcrumbs along the way.

And finally, I am grateful to Connor Wolfe and Wayfarer Books for believing in my work, and continuing to ensure that the mainstream isn't the only stream.

Endnotes

1   Stafford, Kim. *The Muses Among Us*. University of Georgia Press: Athens, GA, 2003, p. 13.

2   Blackie, Sharon. *Hagitude.* New World Library: Novato, CA, 2022, p. 238.

3   Sund, Robert. *Poems from Ish River Country*. Shoemaker & Hoard: Washington, D.C., 2004, preface.

4   Durham, Heather. *Going Feral: Field Notes on Wonder and Wanderlust.* Trail to Table Press: Eastsound, WA, 2019.

5   Durham, Heather. *Wolf Tree: An Ecopsychological Memoir in Essays.* Homebound Publications: Stonington, CT, 2022.

6   Mark, Joshua J., "Cats in the Ancient World." *Ancient History Encyclopedia*, 17 November 2012. https://www.ancient.eu/article/466/cats-in-the-ancient-world/

7   Dillard, Annie. *Pilgrim at Tinker Creek*. Harper & Row: New York, NY, 1974. P. 181.

8   Ibid. p. 182.

9   Ibid. p. 205.

10   Ibid. p. 217.

11   Oliver, Mary. "Praying." *Devotions,* Penguin Press: New York, NY, 2017, p. 131.

12   Hodgson, Derek. "How Did Reading and Writing Evolve?" *Cosmos Magazine,* 11 March 2019. https://cosmos-magazine.com/people/how-did-reading-and-writing-evolve-neuroscience-gives-a-clue/

13   Doyle, Brian. *The Adventures of John Carson in Several Quarters of the World: A Novel of Robert Louis Stevenson*, Thomas Dunne Books: New York, NY, 2017, p. 192.

14   BPD and related resources I've personally found helpful:

https://www.borderlinepersonalitydisorder.org

https://www.nimh.nih.gov/health/topics/borderline-personality-disorder

Aguirre, Blaise, and Gillian Galen. *Mindfulness for Borderline Personality Disorder*. New Harbinger Publications Inc., 2013

Chapman, Alexander, and Kim Gratz. *The Borderline Personality Disorder Survival Guide*. New Harbinger Publications Inc., 2007

McKay, Matthew, Jeffrey Wood, and Jeffrey Brantley. *The Dialectical Behavior Therapy Skills Workbook*. New Harbinger Publications Inc., 2019

Porges, Stephen. *The Pocket Guide to the Polyvagal Theory.* W.W. Norton & Co., 2017

15   Dillard, Annie. *Pilgrim at Tinker Creek*. Harper & Row: New York, NY, 1974. p. 248.

about the author

Heather Durham holds degrees in psychology, ecology, and creative nonfiction, though her formal writing is rooted in journaling, and her journaling rooted in wandering, wondering, and attempting to make sense. As an introspective introvert, she's continually sought meaning and belonging within natural communities, and has come to understand nature connection as her primary relationship, capable of holding and healing all others.

Heather grew up in New England, wandered widely, and finds herself in midlife rooting firmly in the land of ravens and salmon, on the traditional lands of Snohomish, Snoqualmie, and other Coast Salish tribes, amidst the towering cedars and moody mists of the Pacific Northwest. When not working or writing, you are likely to find Heather out birding with friends; reading memoirs, essay collections, or ecopsychology texts; or hunkered down in a creekside cedar grove with a journal, field guide, and binoculars, remembering wildness.

Learn more at heatherdurhamauthor.com.

WAYFARER

BASED IN ABIQUIU, NEW MEXICO

At Wayfarer Books we believe poetry is the language of the earth. We believe words— shaped like rivers through wild places—can change the shape of the world. We publish poets and writers and renegades who stand outside of mainstream culture—poets, essayists, and storytellers whose work might withstand the scrutiny of crows and coyotes, those who are cryptic and floral, the crepuscular, and the queer-at-heart. We are more than just a publisher but a community of writers. Our mission is to produce books that can serve as a compass and map to all wayfarers through wild terrain.

WAYFARERBOOKS.ORG

www.ingramcontent.com/pod-product-compliance
Lightning Source LLC
Chambersburg PA
CBHW020242130626
46549CB00005B/2017